Practical Rust 1.x Cookbook

100+ Solutions across Command Line, CI/CD, Kubernetes, Networking, Code Performance and Microservices

Rustacean Team

Contents

PREFACE

Practical Rust 1.x Cookbook is an in-depth guide for experienced Rust programmers looking to create robust and efficient applications. This solution-focused book covers a wide range of topics, including command-line, webassembly, networking, kubernetes, microservices, and system programming.

This book includes over 100 real-world practical exercises that will teach you how to use the Rust compiler and command-line programming across every stage of software development. Each exercise is intended to reinforce Rust's potential for outperforming legacy applications and bridging the high performance gap. You'll learn about advanced solutions like asynchronous functions, API testing, CI/CD pipelines, Fuzz testing, and microservices architecture as you read the book. You'll also have the chance to put your knowledge to use by solving complex concurrent and parallel code challenges. You'll also get hands-on experience with many of Rust's built-in frameworks and libraries.

Practical Rust 1.x Cookbook is a must-have for both experienced and inexperienced Rust programmers looking to create high-performance and robust applications. This book will help you stay ahead of the curve in Rust coding by providing clear explanations, practical examples, and step-by-step illustrations. Get your copy today and start making the apps you've always wanted to make!

This book will teach you how to:
- Employing declarative and procedural macros, pattern matching, and enums
- Create and test asynchronous code, error handling, and communication patterns.
- Working with deadlocks and livelocks, as well as implementing hash maps and parallel algorithms
- SOAP and REST API development, API orchestration, and performance monitoring
- API layering, middleware programming, and end-to-end API testing
- CI/CD, Docker registry, Kubernetes cluster, YAML files, and load balancers configuration
- Working with fuzz testing, checking syntax, and identifying code vulnerabilities

This book is written by a team of Rust professionals with an intent to contribute and return back to both industry and academic research communities.

GitforGits

Prerequisites

This book assumes you have already begun with rust programming and working towards building error-free, robust and scalable programs. Rust is a modern, safe and efficient systems programming language that is widely used in industry and is a good choice for developers who want to build high-performance, concurrent, and safe systems.

Codes Usage

Are you in need of some helpful code examples to assist you in your programming and documentation? Look no further! Our book offers a wealth of supplemental material, including code examples and exercises.

Not only is this book here to aid you in getting your job done, but you have our permission to use the example code in your programs and documentation. However, please note that if you are reproducing a significant portion of the code, we do require you to contact us for Permission.

But don't worry, using several chunks of code from this book in your program or answering a question by citing our book and quoting example code does not require permission. But if you do choose to give credit, an attribution typically includes the title, author, publisher, and ISBN. For example, "Practical Rust 1.x Cookbook by the Rustacean Team".

If you are unsure whether your intended use of the code examples falls under fair use or the permissions outlined above, please do not hesitate to reach out to us at kittenpub.kdp@gmail.com.

We are happy to assist and clarify any concerns.

Acknowledgement

The Rustacean team would express their gratitude to all of the other contributors to Rust and work tirelessly to improve the quality of the programming language. While they are doing this, they would want to express their gratitude to the copywriters, tech editors, and reviewers who helped create a powerful yet simple book that outperforms rust coding in a relatively short period of time.

CHAPTER 1: SETTING UP AND CONFIGURING RUST ENVIRONMENT

Recipe#1: Installing Rust Compiler

What Does Rust Compiler Do?

The Rust compiler is a piece of software that takes the source code written in Rust and converts it into machine code so that it can be run on a computer. The syntax and semantics of the source code are both validated by the Rust compiler to ensure that the code is accurate and well-formed. The executable file that contains the programme written in machine code will be generated by the compiler if the source code is correct.

Because it enables developers to write code in a high-level language and then have it translated into machine code that can be run on a computer, the Rust compiler is an essential component of the Rust development process. Rust is a computer programming language that was created by Mozilla. It also offers a number of additional features, such as error checking and optimization, to assist developers in writing high-quality code, and it does this in a number of different ways.

Install Rust Compiler and Tools

To install the Rust compiler and tools, you can follow these steps:

- Download the Rust installer: You can download the Rust installer from the Rust website (https://www.rust-lang.org/). The installer is available for Windows, macOS, and Linux. You can follow the below steps -
    - Go to the Rust website (https://www.rust-lang.org/).
    - Click the "Download" button in the top right corner of the page.
    - Select the installer for your operating system (Windows, macOS, or Linux).
    - Download the installer by clicking the "Download Rust" button.
- Run the installer: Once the installer has downloaded, you can run it to begin the installation process. Follow the below steps -
    - Once the download is complete, open the installer file.

- ○ Follow the prompts to install the Rust compiler and tools. This may include accepting a license agreement, choosing an installation location, and installing any additional dependencies.

- Verify the installation: Once the installation is complete, you can verify the installation by opening a terminal or command prompt and running the rustc --version command. This should output the version of the Rust compiler that is installed on your machine. Alternatively, you can install rustup along with rust as below -
  - ○ Go to the Rust website (https://www.rust-lang.org/).
  - ○ Click the "Download" button in the top right corner of the page.
  - ○ Scroll down to the "Install with rustup" section.
  - ○ Click the "Install" button for your operating system (Windows, macOS, or Linux).
  - ○ This will download the rustup-init script to your machine.
  - ○ Open a terminal or command prompt.
  - ○ Navigate to the directory where you downloaded the rustup-init script.
  - ○ Run the rustup-init script by typing ./rustup-init and pressing Enter.
  - ○ Follow the prompts to install rustup. This may include accepting a license agreement and choosing an installation location.
  - ○ Once the installation is complete, you can verify the installation by running the rustup --version command. This should output the version of rustup that is installed on your machine.

That's it! You should now have rustup installed and ready to use. You can use rustup to install and manage different versions of Rust and its associated tools. For example, you can use the rustup install command to install a specific version of Rust, or the rustup default command to set a default version of Rust to use.

Recipe#2: Creating a New Rust Project

Files and Directories

A collection of files and directories that contain Rust source code and any other resources that may be associated with it, such as configuration files and dependencies, is referred to as a Rust project. The cargo build system is a tool for building, testing, and managing Rust projects. This system is typically used to organize Rust projects, and it is referred to as the cargo build system.

Developing a Rust project is essential because it offers a framework that can be utilized for the purpose of arranging and constructing your Rust code. You will be able to use the cargo tool to build and run your code, as well as specify dependencies and build configurations. Sharing your code with other people and managing multiple Rust projects both become less difficult as a result of this.

The cargo new command can be used to initiate the creation of a new Rust project. This command will populate the new project directory with all of the essential files and directories. After that, you can implement your project by editing the Rust source code files that are located in the src directory. After that, you can use the cargo commands to build and run your code.

Setting Up Rust Project After Installation

To create a new Rust project after installing Rust, you can follow these steps:
- Open a terminal or command prompt.
- Navigate to the directory where you want to create your Rust project.
- Run the cargo new command, followed by the name of your project and any desired options. For example:

```
cargo new my-project
```

This will create a new directory with the specified name, and generate the necessary files and directories for a new Rust project. The most important file is Cargo.toml, which specifies the project's dependencies and build configuration.

- Navigate to the project directory by running:

```
cd my-project
```

You can now edit the Rust source code files in the src directory to implement your project.

- To build and run the project, you can use the cargo build and cargo run commands, respectively. For example:

```
cargo build
cargo run
```

If your project depends on external crates or libraries, you can add them to your Cargo.toml file by specifying them as dependencies. This will ensure that they are installed and available to your project when it is built.

That's it! You should now have a basic Rust project set up and ready to go. You can continue developing and debugging your project as needed.

Recipe#3: Managing Dependencies to Your Project

What are Dependencies?

Your Rust project must have a certain number of dependencies, which can be thought of as external crates or libraries, in order for it to successfully build and run. Additional functionality, such as networking or serialisation, that is not included in the Rust standard library can be provided by dependencies.

Dependencies are required for a Rust project because they enable you to incorporate code written in other languages or by other developers. This not only prevents you from having to reimplement functionality that is already present, but it also gives you access to specialised libraries and tools that are not included in the standard library. This can save you a lot of time and effort.

Following are some helpful examples of dependencies that you might use in a Rust project:
- reqwest: A library for making HTTP requests in Rust.
- serde: A library for serializing and deserializing data in Rust.
- tokio: A library for building asynchronous applications in Rust.
- clap: A library for parsing command-line arguments in Rust.

To use a dependency in your Rust project, you need to specify it in your Cargo.toml file and then import the necessary items from the dependency in your Rust code. cargo will automatically download and install the dependency when you build your project.

How to Add/Remove/Modify Dependencies?

To manage dependencies to a Rust project, you can follow these steps:
- Open the Cargo.toml file in your project directory. This file specifies the dependencies and build configuration for your project.
- Under the [dependencies] section, add a line for each dependency you want to include. Each line should specify the name of the dependency and the version you want to use, separated by an = sign. For example:

```
[dependencies]
reqwest = "0.10.8"
tokio = "0.2.22"
```

- Save the Cargo.toml file.

- Run the cargo build command to build your project. This will cause cargo to download and install any specified dependencies, and then build your project using those dependencies.
- If you want to update or remove a dependency, you can edit the Cargo.toml file accordingly and run the cargo build command again to update the dependencies in your project.

That's it! You should now have your desired dependencies included in your Rust project. You can use them in your Rust code by adding extern crate declarations and importing the necessary items from the dependencies.

For example, to add dependencies to a Rust project, you can use the cargo add command. This command allows you to add new dependencies to your Cargo.toml file and install them in your project. For example, to add the serde library as a dependency, you can run the following command:

cargo add serde

To remove dependencies from a Rust project, you can use the cargo remove command. This command removes the dependency from the Cargo.toml file and uninstalls it from the project. For example, to remove the serde library as a dependency, you can run the following command:

cargo remove serde

To modify dependencies in a Rust project, you can edit the Cargo.toml file directly. This file lists all of the dependencies for the project, along with their version numbers. You can change the version numbers or add/remove dependencies as needed. For example, to update the version of the serde library to the latest version, you can modify the Cargo.toml file as follows:

[dependencies]
serde = "1.0"

[dependencies]
serde = "1.1"

After making any changes to the Cargo.toml file, you will need to run cargo build or cargo run to rebuild the project with the updated dependencies.

Recipe#4: Installing Visual Studio Code IDE for Rust

Understanding VS Code IDE

Visual Studio Code (VS Code) is a free and open-source code editor developed by Microsoft. It is a powerful and feature-rich code editor that is widely used by developers to write and debug code. It is available for Windows, Linux, and macOS.

VS Code includes a built-in terminal, code debugging, integrated Git support, code snippets, and a wide range of extensions to add additional functionality. It supports many programming languages and has a syntax highlighting feature that helps to make code easier to read. It is also highly customizable, so you can customize the interface and change settings to suit your workflow.

Benefits of VS Code IDE for Rust Users

There are several benefits of using Visual Studio Code (VS Code) as an Integrated Development Environment (IDE) for Rust programming:

- Syntax highlighting: VS Code has excellent support for Rust syntax highlighting, which makes it easy to read and write Rust code.
- Debugging: VS Code has a built-in debugger that allows you to set breakpoints, inspect variables, and step through code.
- Code completion: VS Code has IntelliSense, a feature that provides code completion suggestions as you type. This can save you time and improve your productivity.

- Formatting: VS Code has an automatic code formatting feature that helps to keep your code organized and easy to read.
- Git integration: VS Code has built-in support for Git, allowing you to easily manage your version control from within the editor.
- Extension ecosystem: VS Code has a large ecosystem of extensions that can add additional functionality to the editor. There are extensions available for Rust that provide additional features such as code snippets, linting, and integration with popular Rust tools.

Overall, VS Code is a feature-rich and powerful IDE that is well-suited for Rust development.

Why VS Code IDE for Rust?

Visual Studio Code (VS Code) is a popular cross-platform code editor that includes support for Rust development. Some benefits of using VS Code for Rust include:

Syntax highlighting: VS Code includes syntax highlighting for Rust code, which can make it easier to read and write code by highlighting different elements such as keywords, variables, and functions.

Code completion: VS Code includes code completion for Rust, which can help you write code faster by suggesting possible completions as you type.

Debugging: VS Code includes debugging support for Rust, which allows you to set breakpoints, inspect variables, and step through code to help identify and fix issues.

Integrated terminal: VS Code includes an integrated terminal that allows you to run cargo and other command-line tools directly from the editor.

Extension marketplace: VS Code has a large extension marketplace that includes a number of extensions specifically designed for Rust development, such as Rust Analyzer and Rust symbol completion.

Overall, VS Code is a powerful and user-friendly IDE that can make Rust development more efficient and enjoyable.

Steps to Install VS Code

To install Visual Studio Code (VS Code) for Rust development, you can follow these steps:

- Go to the Visual Studio Code website (https://code.visualstudio.com/).
- Click the "Download" button to download the VS Code installer for your operating system (Windows, macOS, or Linux).
- Once the download is complete, open the installer file.
- Follow the prompts to install VS Code. This may include accepting a license agreement and choosing an installation location.
- Once the installation is complete, open VS Code.
- To install the Rust extension for VS Code, click the "Extensions" icon in the left-hand side menu, or press Ctrl+Shift+X (Windows) or Cmd+Shift+X (macOS).
- In the search bar at the top of the extensions window, search for "Rust".
- Click the "Install" button for the "Rust (rls)" extension.
- Once the extension is installed, you may be prompted to install the Rust compiler and tools. If so, follow the prompts to install Rust.
- To verify that the Rust extension is installed and working correctly, you can create a new Rust file (e.g. main.rs) and write some Rust code. The syntax highlighting and code completion should work as expected.

That's it! You should now have Visual Studio Code installed and configured for Rust development. You can use it to edit and debug your Rust code, and use the integrated terminal to run cargo and other command-line tools.

Recipe#5: Supporting Non-Rust Tools and Libraries

List of Non-Rust Libraries and Packages

There are many non-Rust libraries and packages that support Rust development. Here is a list of some popular ones:

- Reqwest: A Rust library for making HTTP requests.
- Serde: A Rust library for serializing and deserializing data.
- Tokiio: A Rust library for building asynchronous applications.
- Clap: A Rust library for parsing command-line arguments.
- NumPy: A Python library for scientific computing that includes support for Rust through the pyo3 crate.
- PostgreSQL: A database management system that includes support for Rust through the postgres crate.
- GTK: A GUI toolkit that includes support for Rust through the gtk crate.
- OpenCV: A computer vision library that includes support for Rust through the opencv crate.
- Diesel: A Rust library for interacting with databases.
- Hyper: A Rust library for writing HTTP clients and servers.
- Rustls: A Rust library for TLS (Transport Layer Security).
- RabbitMQ: A message broker that includes support for Rust through the amqp crate.
- Protobuf: A serialization library that includes support for Rust through the prost crate.
- FFmpeg: A multimedia framework that includes support for Rust through the av crate.
- LLVM: A compiler infrastructure that includes support for Rust through the llvm-sys crate.
- OpenGL: A graphics library that includes support for Rust through the glium crate.

These libraries and packages can be used to add various functionality to your Rust projects, such as networking, database access, GUI development, and multimedia processing. They can be included as dependencies in your Cargo.toml file and imported in your Rust code to make use of their functionality.

Step-By-Step to Load and Implement Non-Rust Libraries

To load and implement non-Rust libraries into a Rust project, you can follow these steps:
- Determine the name and version of the library you want to use. This information should be available in the library's documentation.
- Open the Cargo.toml file in your Rust project directory. This file specifies the dependencies and build configuration for your project.
- Under the [dependencies] section, add a line for the library you want to use. The line should specify the name of the library and the version you want to use, separated by an = sign. For example:

```
[dependencies]
reqwest = "0.10.8"
```

- Save the Cargo.toml file.
- In your Rust code, add an extern crate declaration for the library at the top of the file where you want to use it. For example:

```
extern crate reqwest;
```

- Use the use keyword to import the necessary items from the library. For example:

```
use reqwest::Client;
```

- You can now use the library in your Rust code by calling functions or methods from the imported items.
- Run the cargo build command to build your project. This will cause cargo to download and install the specified dependency, and then build your project using the dependency.

If you encounter any errors while building or using the library, you may need to consult the library's documentation or seek assistance from the library's authors or community.

If you want to update or remove the dependency, you can edit the Cargo.toml file accordingly and run the cargo build command again to update the dependency in your project.

Recipe#6: Setting Up Code Testing Tools

List of Various Code Testing Tools

Code testing tools are used to verify that code is working correctly and meets certain requirements or expectations. They are needed because they help ensure that code is reliable and of high quality, and can help catch bugs and other issues before they become problems in production.

In Rust, there are several popular code testing tools available:

- cargo test: This is a built-in command in the cargo build tool that allows you to run tests for your Rust project. Tests are specified in special test files in the tests directory of your project, and can be run using the cargo test command.
- assert_eq!: This is a macro in the Rust standard library that allows you to assert that two values are equal. It can be used in test functions to verify that the output of a function or expression is as expected.
- assert!: This is a macro in the Rust standard library that allows you to assert that a boolean expression is true. It can be used in test functions to verify that certain conditions are met.
- quickcheck: This is a Rust library that provides support for automated property-based testing. It allows you to specify properties that should hold for a piece of code, and then generates random inputs to test those properties.
- proptest: This is a Rust library that provides advanced support for property-based testing. It

allows you to specify complex properties and constraints, and provides a range of features for debugging and minimizing failing test cases.

These are just a few examples of the code testing tools available in Rust. There are many more available, each with their own strengths and features. You can choose the testing tools that best fit your needs and workflow.

Install and Configure Code Testing Tools

To install and configure code testing tools in a Rust project, you can follow these steps:

- Make sure you have the cargo build tool installed on your system. If you don't have it installed, you can install it by following the instructions at https://www.rust-lang.org/tools/install.
- Create a new Rust project or open an existing one.
- To add the assert_eq! and assert! macros to your project, you will need to include the std crate in your code. You can do this by adding an extern crate std declaration at the top of the file where you want to use the macros.
- To use the assert_eq! macro, you can call it with two arguments: the expected value and the actual value. For example:

```
assert_eq!(2 + 2, 4);
```

- To use the assert! macro, you can call it with a boolean expression as an argument. For example:

```
assert!(2 + 2 == 4);
```

- To add the quickcheck library to your project, you will need to add it as a dependency in your Cargo.toml file. You can do this by adding a line under the [dependencies] section like this:

```
quickcheck = "0.10.0"
```

- To use quickcheck, you will need to include it in your code by adding an extern crate quickcheck declaration at the top of the file where you want to use it.
- To write a property-based test using quickcheck, you will need to define a function with the #[quickcheck] attribute and specify the inputs and output as function arguments. For example:

```
#[quickcheck]
fn sum_is_greater_than_its_parts(x: i32, y: i32) -> bool {
    x + y > x && x + y > y
}
```

- To add the proptest library to your project, you will need to add it as a dependency in your Cargo.toml file. You can do this by adding a line under the [dependencies] section like this:

```
proptest = "0.10.0"
```

- To use proptest, you will need to include it in your code by adding an extern crate proptest declaration at the top of the file where you want to use it.
- To write a property-based test using proptest, you will need to define a function with the #[proptest] attribute and specify the inputs and output as function arguments. You can use the proptest! macro to specify the test case and any constraints or configuration options. For example:

```
#[proptest]
fn    sum_is_greater_than_its_parts(x:    i32,    y:    i32)    ->
prop::TestResult {
    prop::proptest!(|(x, y)| {
        assert!(x + y > x && x + y > y);
    })
}
```

- To run your tests, you can use the cargo test command. This will build your project and run all of the tests in the tests directory. You can also specify the name of a specific test function to run just that test.

That's it! You should now have code testing tools installed and configured in your Rust project. You can use these tools to write and run tests for your code, and verify that it is working correctly and meeting your requirements.

Recipe#7: Installing and Configuring Cargo

What is Cargo?

Cargo is Rust's build system and package manager. with this tool, you'll get a repeatable build because it allows Rust packages to declare their dependencies in the manifest, Cargo.toml. When you install Rust through rustup, Cargo is also installed.

Cargo allows Rust packages to declare their dependencies. This is done in the Cargo.toml file. All you have to do is declare the dependencies required to run your program in the Cargo.toml file. Next, Cargo extracts all the necessary information about your dependencies and build information into the Cargo.lock file.

The function of the Cargo.lock file is to allow for a repeatable build. Therefore, there should be no cases of different builds, even when you share your project.

You may be wondering how the Cargo.toml and Cargo.lock files are different. Cargo.toml is a manifest, which is a document that contains detailed information about passengers, goods, etc. In Rust, the manifest contains detailed information about a given project, such as the project name, version, dependencies, etc. The manifest tells Cargo which dependency it needs to download to compile your project successfully.

Install Cargo Package Manager

To install Cargo, the official build and package manager for Rust, you can follow these steps:

- Make sure you have Rust installed on your system. You can check if Rust is already installed by running the rustc --version command. If Rust is not installed, you can install it by following the instructions at https://www.rust-lang.org/tools/install.
- Cargo is distributed with Rust, so you don't need to install it separately. However, you may need to update it to the latest version if it is out of date. To update Cargo, run the following command:

```
cargo install cargo-update
```

- Once Cargo is updated, you can use it to manage your Rust projects. To create a new Rust project with Cargo, run the following command:

```
cargo new myproject
```

- This will create a new directory called myproject with the basic files and directories needed for a Rust project, including a Cargo.toml file that specifies the dependencies and build configuration for the project.
- To build and run your project, you can use the cargo build and cargo run commands, respectively. For example:

```
cargo build
cargo run
```

You can also use Cargo to manage dependencies, run tests, and perform other tasks related to your Rust project. for more information, you can refer to the Cargo documentation at https://doc.rust-lang.org/cargo/.

Step-By-Step Configuring Cargo

To configure Cargo, the official build and package manager for Rust, you can follow these steps:

- Make sure you have Cargo installed on your system. You can check if Cargo is already installed by running the cargo --version command. If Cargo is not installed, you can install it by following the instructions at https://www.rust-lang.org/tools/install.
- To configure Cargo, you will need to edit the Cargo.toml file in your Rust project directory. This file specifies the dependencies and build configuration for your project.
- The Cargo.toml file has several sections that you can use to configure your project. Some of the most important ones are:

[package]: This section specifies metadata about your project, such as the name, version, and authors.

[dependencies]: This section specifies the dependencies for your project. You can add dependencies by specifying the name and version of the crate, like this:

```
[dependencies]
reqwest = "0.10.8"
```

[dev-dependencies]: This section specifies dependencies that are only needed for development and testing, but not for production.

[build-dependencies]: This section specifies dependencies that are needed for building your project, but not for running it.

[features]: This section allows you to enable or disable optional features of your project.

- Once you have edited the Cargo.toml file to specify the desired configuration for your project, you can use the cargo build command to build your project with the new configuration.
- You can also use the cargo check command to check your project for errors and warnings

without building it, or the cargo run command to build and run your project.

CHAPTER 2: HANDS-ON TRAITS, ENUMS AND STRUCT

There are a number of essential concepts and features that are important to know when coding in Rust. Some of the most important ones include:

- Ownership and borrowing: Rust has a unique ownership and borrowing system that allows you to specify which parts of your code have access to which data. This helps ensure that data is used safely and efficiently, and can help prevent common programming errors such as null or dangling pointer references.
- Traits: Traits are a way to define generic behavior in Rust. They allow you to specify a set of methods that a type must implement, and can be used to abstract over different types in a flexible and reusable way.
- Enums: Enums (enumerations) are a way to define a type that can have a fixed set of values. They can be used to represent a choice between a finite set of options, and can be used in pattern matching to perform different actions depending on the value of an enum.
- Structs: Structs are a way to define a custom data type in Rust. They allow you to group related data together into a single entity, and can be used to define complex data structures such as trees or graphs.
- Matching: Matching is a powerful and expressive way to control the flow of execution in Rust. It allows you to match a value against a set of patterns and execute different code depending on which pattern matches.
- Concurrency: Rust has strong support for concurrent programming, with features such as threads, channels, and the async/await syntax. These features allow you to write code that can run concurrently and communicate with each other, enabling you to take advantage of multiple CPU cores and write efficient, parallel code.
- Unsafe code: Rust has a strong emphasis on safety and correctness, but sometimes it is necessary to write code that bypasses the borrow checker and other safety checks. This is known as "unsafe" code, and should be used with caution as it can introduce vulnerabilities and other risks.
- Macros: Rust has a powerful macro system that allows you to define custom code transformations at compile-time. Macros can be used to generate code, define custom syntax, or perform other tasks that would be difficult or impractical to do using regular Rust code.
- Modules: Modules are a way to organize and encapsulate your code in Rust. They allow you

to divide your code into logical units and control visibility and access to different parts of your code.

- Cargo: Cargo is the official build and package manager for Rust. It provides a convenient way to build, test, and publish Rust projects, and is an essential tool for any Rust developer.

These are just a few examples of the essential concepts and features that are important to know when coding in Rust. There are many more to learn and explore, and you will discover and learn new things as you continue to work with Rust.

Recipe#1: Working with Traits

How to Declare Traits?

In Rust, you can define a trait by using the trait keyword and specifying the associated types, functions, and other items that the trait defines. Following is a sample program on how you might define a trait in Rust:

```
trait MyTrait {
    type Output;
    fn do_something(&self) -> Self::Output;
}
```

In this example, MyTrait is a trait that defines an associated type Output and a method do_something() that takes a reference to self and returns a value of type Self::Output. The Self keyword refers to the type that is implementing the trait, and the Output associated type refers to the type that is associated with the implementing type.

To implement a trait for a type, you can use the impl keyword and specify the type and the trait, like this:

```rust
struct MyStruct;

impl MyTrait for MyStruct {
    type Output = i32;
    fn do_something(&self) -> Self::Output {
        42
    }
}
```

In this example, we are implementing MyTrait for the MyStruct type. We specify that the Output associated type is i32, and we implement the do_something() method to return the value 42.

Execute a Trait for Struct

To implement a trait for a type in Rust, you can use the impl keyword and specify the type and the trait, like this:

```rust
struct MyStruct;

impl MyTrait for MyStruct {
    type Output = i32;
    fn do_something(&self) -> Self::Output {
        42
    }
}
```

In this example, we are implementing the MyTrait trait for the MyStruct type. We specify that the Output associated type is i32, and we implement the do_something() method to return the value 42.

You can implement a trait for a type as many times as you like, as long as the trait is fully implemented for that type. You can also implement a trait for a type multiple times with different associated types or method implementations, as long as the different implementations have different generic type parameters.

Following is a sample program on how you might implement a trait multiple times for the same type:

```rust
struct MyStruct;

impl MyTrait for MyStruct {
    type Output = i32;
    fn do_something(&self) -> Self::Output {
        42
    }
}

impl MyTrait for MyStruct {
    type Output = bool;
    fn do_something(&self) -> Self::Output {
        true
    }
}
```

In this example, we have implemented MyTrait twice for the MyStruct type, with different associated types and method implementations. The first implementation has an Output associated type of i32 and returns the value 42, while the second implementation has an Output associated type of bool and returns the value true.

Implement Different Types of Traits

To implement different types of traits for a type in Rust, you can use the impl keyword and specify the type and the trait, like this:

```rust
struct MyStruct;

impl MyTrait1 for MyStruct {
    type Output = i32;
    fn do_something(&self) -> Self::Output {
        42
    }
}

impl MyTrait2 for MyStruct {
    fn do_something_else(&self) {
        println!("Doing something else");
    }
}
```

In this example, we are implementing the MyTrait1 and MyTrait2 traits for the MyStruct type. The MyTrait1 trait defines an associated type Output and a method do_something(), while the MyTrait2 trait defines a method do_something_else(). We implement these methods for the MyStruct type as needed.

You can implement as many different types of traits for a type as you like, as long as the traits are fully implemented for that type. You can also implement the same trait multiple times for a type with different associated types or method implementations, as long as the different implementations have different generic type parameters.

Following is a sample program on how you might implement multiple traits for the same type:

```rust
struct MyStruct;

impl MyTrait1 for MyStruct {
    type Output = i32;
    fn do_something(&self) -> Self::Output {
        42
```

```
    }
}

impl MyTrait2 for MyStruct {
    fn do_something_else(&self) {
        println!("Doing something else");
    }
}

impl MyTrait3 for MyStruct {
fn do_something_else_again(&self) {
println!("Doing something else again");
}
}
```

In this example, we have implemented three different traits for the MyStruct type: MyTrait1, MyTrait2, and MyTrait3. Each trait defines a different set of methods and associated types, and we have implemented these methods and types for the MyStruct type as needed.

Recipe#2: Define Function Inside Traits

Define Function Inside a Trait

In Rust, you can define functions inside a trait to specify the behavior that must be implemented by any type that implements the trait. To write a function inside a trait, you can use the fn keyword and specify the function signature, like this:

```
trait MyTrait {
    fn do_something(&self) -> i32;
}
```

In this example, MyTrait is a trait that defines a function do_something() that takes a reference to self and returns an i32 value.

Implement Function Within a Trait

To implement a function inside a trait for a type, you can use the impl keyword and specify the type and the trait, like this:

```rust
struct MyStruct;

impl MyTrait for MyStruct {
    fn do_something(&self) -> i32 {
        42
    }
}
```

In this example, we are implementing the do_something() function for the MyStruct type. We implement the function by specifying the body of the function, which in this case is a simple return statement that returns the value 42.

You can define as many functions inside a trait as you like, and you can implement them for a type as needed. You can also define generic functions inside a trait, which allow you to abstract over different types in a flexible and reusable way.

Declare Generic Functions Inside a Trait

Following is a sample program on how you might define a generic function inside a trait:

```rust
trait MyTrait<T> {
    fn do_something_with<U>(&self, value: U) -> (T, U);
}
```

```rust
struct MyStruct<T> {
    value: T,
}


impl<T> MyTrait<T> for MyStruct<T> {
    fn do_something_with<U>(&self, value: U) -> (T, U) {
        (self.value, value)
    }
}
```

In this example, MyTrait is a trait that defines a generic function do_something_with() that takes a reference to self and a value of type U, and returns a tuple of type (T, U), where T is the type parameter of the trait and U is the type parameter of the function. We implement the trait for the MyStruct type, which also has a type parameter T, and we specify the body of the function to return a tuple containing the value of self.value and the value of value.

Recipe#3: How to Define Enums

Define Enums

In Rust, you can define enums (enumerations) using the enum keyword, like this:

```rust
enum MyEnum {
    Value1,
    Value2,
    Value3,
}
```

In this example, MyEnum is an enum with three variant values: Value1, Value2, and Value3. Each variant represents a different value that the enum can take.

Implement Enums

You can implement enums in the same way as any other type in Rust, using the impl keyword and specifying the enum and the trait or methods you want to implement. Following is a sample program on how you might implement a trait for an enum:

```
impl MyTrait for MyEnum {
    fn do_something(&self) -> i32 {
        match self {
            MyEnum::Value1 => 1,
            MyEnum::Value2 => 2,
            MyEnum::Value3 => 3,
        }
    }
}
```

In this example, we are implementing the MyTrait trait for the MyEnum enum. We do this by using a match expression to match on the variant value of self and return a different value depending on which variant is matched.

Fix Common Issues with Enums

If you encounter issues with enums, one common problem is trying to use a variant value that has not been defined in the enum. To fix this, you can either define the missing variant value in the enum, or you can use a _ wildcard pattern to handle any variant values that are not explicitly matched.

For example:

```
enum MyEnum {
```

```
    Value1,
    Value2,
    Value3,
}

let x = MyEnum::Value4; // error: variant `Value4` not defined
in `MyEnum`

match x {
    MyEnum::Value1 => println!("Value1"),
    MyEnum::Value2 => println!("Value2"),
    MyEnum::Value3 => println!("Value3"),
    _ => println!("Other value"),
}
```

In this example, we are trying to match on the value of x, which is an instance of the MyEnum enum. However, x has the value MyEnum::Value4, which is not defined in the enum. This will cause a compile-time error.

To fix this issue, we can either define the Value4 variant in the MyEnum enum, or we can use a wildcard pattern _ to handle any variant values that are not explicitly matched. This will allow the code to compile and run without an error.

Recipe#4: Tips and Considerations Regarding Enums

Declare Variant Values with Types and Fields

You can define variant values with different types, like this:

```
enum MyEnum {
    Value1(i32),
    Value2(String),
}
```

In this example, the Value1 variant has the type i32, while the Value2 variant has the type String.

You can define variant values with fields, like this:

```
enum MyEnum {
    Value1 { x: i32, y: i32 },
    Value2 { s: String },
}
```

In this example, the Value1 variant has two fields x and y of type i32, while the Value2 variant has a single field s of type String.

Pattern Match with 'match' Expression

You can use the match expression to pattern match on variant values and fields, like this:

```
let x = MyEnum::Value1 { x: 1, y: 2 };

match x {
    MyEnum::Value1 { x, y } => println!("x = {}, y = {}", x, y),
    MyEnum::Value2 { s } => println!("s = {}", s),
}
```

In this example, we are using the match expression to pattern match on the value of x. If x has the Value1 variant, we match on the x and y fields and print their values. If x has the Value2 variant, we match on the s field and print its value.

Use of If Let Expressions

You can use the if let expression to match on a single variant value and bind its fields to variables, like this:

```
let x = MyEnum::Value1 { x: 1, y: 2 };
```

You can use the #[derive()] attribute to automatically generate implementations of common traits for your enums. For example, you can use the #[derive(PartialEq, Eq)] attribute to generate implementations of the PartialEq and Eq traits for your enum, which allow you to compare and test for equality between enum values.

```
#[derive(PartialEq, Eq)]
enum MyEnum {
    Value1,
    Value2,
}

let x = MyEnum::Value1;
let y = MyEnum::Value2;

assert!(x != y);
```

In this example, we have derived the PartialEq and Eq traits for the MyEnum enum. This allows us to use the != operator to compare the values of x and y, and to use the assert!() macro to test for equality.

You can use the enum keyword to define a "c-like" enum, which is a named collection of integer constants. For example:

```rust
enum MyEnum {
    Value1 = 1,
    Value2 = 2,
    Value3 = 3,
}

let x = MyEnum::Value1;

assert_eq!(x as i32, 1);
```

In this example, we have defined an enum MyEnum with three variant values Value1, Value2, and Value3, each of which is associated with a specific integer value. We can use the as operator to cast the value of x to an i32 and test its value using the assert_eq!() macro.

Recipe#5: Parsing and Interpreting Enum Arguments

Why to Parse Arguments?

Parsing arguments refers to the process of extracting and interpreting the input arguments that are passed to a program when it is run. In Rust, you can parse arguments by using the std::env::args() function, which returns an iterator over the command-line arguments of the current program.

Following is a sample program on how you might parse arguments in Rust:

```rust
use std::env;

fn main() {
    let args: Vec<String> = env::args().collect();
```

```rust
    if args.len() < 2 {
        println!("Error: missing argument");
        return;
    }

    let arg = &args[1];

    println!("The first argument is: {}", arg);
}
```

In this example, we are using the env::args() function to get an iterator over the command-line arguments of the current program. We are then using the collect() method to collect the arguments into a vector of String values.

Next, we are checking the length of the args vector to make sure that at least one argument was passed to the program. If no arguments were passed, we print an error message and return from the function.

If there is at least one argument, we get the first argument from the args vector and print it.

You can use this basic approach to parse and interpret the arguments of your program as needed. For example, you might want to use additional if statements or a match expression to handle different types of arguments or to check the values of the arguments.

How to Parse Enum Arguments?

To parse enum arguments in Rust, you can use the from_str() method provided by the std::str::FromStr trait to parse a String value into an instance of your enum.

Following is a sample program on how you might define an enum and implement the FromStr trait to parse enum arguments:

```rust
use std::str::FromStr;

#[derive(Debug)]
enum MyEnum {
    Value1,
    Value2,
    Value3,
}

impl FromStr for MyEnum {
    type Err = String;

    fn from_str(s: &str) -> Result<Self, Self::Err> {
        match s {
            "Value1" => Ok(MyEnum::Value1),
            "Value2" => Ok(MyEnum::Value2),
            "Value3" => Ok(MyEnum::Value3),
            _ => Err("invalid value".to_string()),
        }
    }
}

fn main() {
    let args: Vec<String> = std::env::args().collect();

    if args.len() < 2 {
        println!("Error: missing argument");
        return;
    }

    let arg = &args[1];
    let value = arg.parse::<MyEnum>();
```

```
match value {
    Ok(v) => println!("Parsed value: {:?}", v),
    Err(e) => println!("Error parsing value: {}", e),
    }
}
```

In this example, we have defined an enum MyEnum with three variant values: Value1, Value2, and Value3. We have also implemented the FromStr trait for the MyEnum enum, which provides the from_str() method that can be used to parse a String value into an instance of the enum.

In the from_str() method, we are using a match expression to match on the input s and return the corresponding variant value of the enum if it is a valid value. If the input value is not recognized, we return an error using the Err() method.

In the main() function, we are using the parse() method provided by the FromStr trait to parse the first command-line argument into an instance of the MyEnum enum. We are then using a match expression to handle the Ok and Err cases of the parse() method. If the parsing is successful, we print the parsed value. If it fails, we print an error message.

Steps to Interpret Enum Arguments

To interpret enum arguments in Rust, you can use a match expression or the if let expression to pattern match on the variant values of the enum and perform different actions depending on the variant value.

Following is a sample program on how you might interpret enum arguments in Rust:

```
use std::str::FromStr;

#[derive(Debug)]
enum MyEnum {
    Value1,
    Value2,
```

```rust
    Value3,
}

impl FromStr for MyEnum {
    type Err = String;

    fn from_str(s: &str) -> Result<Self, Self::Err> {
        match s {
            "Value1" => Ok(MyEnum::Value1),
            "Value2" => Ok(MyEnum::Value2),
            "Value3" => Ok(MyEnum::Value3),
            _ => Err("invalid value".to_string()),
        }
    }
}

fn main() {
    let args: Vec<String> = std::env::args().collect();

    if args.len() < 2 {
        println!("Error: missing argument");
        return;
    }

    let arg = &args[1];
    let value = arg.parse::<MyEnum>();

    match value {
        Ok(v) => {
            match v {
                MyEnum::Value1 => println!("Value1"),
                MyEnum::Value2 => println!("Value2"),
                MyEnum::Value3 => println!("Value3"),
            }
```

```
        },
        Err(e) => println!("Error parsing value: {}", e),
    }
}
```

In this example, we have defined an enum MyEnum with three variant values: Value1, Value2, and Value3. We have also implemented the FromStr trait for the MyEnum enum, which provides the from_str() method that can be used to parse a String value into an instance of the enum.

In the main() function, we are using the parse() method provided by the FromStr trait to parse the first command-line argument into an instance of the MyEnum enum. We are then using a match expression to handle the Ok and Err cases of the parse() method. If the parsing is successful, we use another match expression to pattern match on the variant value of the enum and print a message depending on the variant value. If the parsing fails, we print an error message.

You can use this approach to interpret enum arguments and perform different actions depending on the variant value of the enum. For example, you might want to call different functions or set different variables depending on the variant value of the enum.

Recipe#6: Initialize Array of Structs

Define Struct and Arrays of Struct

In Rust, you can define a structure (struct) that consists of a set of fields, each of which has a name and a type. You can then create an array of structures by defining an array with the type of the struct as its element type.

Following is a sample program on how to define a struct and an array of that struct in Rust:

```rust
struct Point {
    x: i32,
    y: i32,
}

let points: [Point; 5] = [
    Point { x: 0, y: 0 },
    Point { x: 1, y: 0 },
    Point { x: 2, y: 0 },
    Point { x: 3, y: 0 },
    Point { x: 4, y: 0 },
];
```

In this example, we define a struct named Point that has two fields, x and y, both of which are of type i32. We then define an array named points that has a length of 5 and is made up of elements of type Point.

Initialize Array of Structs Using Loop

To initialize the array, we use a list of Point instances enclosed in square brackets, with each instance being separated by a comma. Each instance is constructed using the Point struct's syntax, which consists of the keyword Point followed by a set of curly braces containing a list of field names and their associated values.

You can also use a loop to initialize the array if the values of the fields are not known beforehand:

```rust
let mut points: [Point; 5] = [Point { x: 0, y: 0 }; 5];

for i in 0..5 {
    points[i] = Point { x: i, y: i * 2 };
}
```

In this example, we use a mutable array (one that can be modified after initialization) and a loop to initialize the x field of each Point element with the loop variable i, and the y field with i * 2.

Initialize Array of Structs Using Trait

You can also use the Default trait to initialize an array of structs with default values. The Default trait is a built-in Rust trait that provides a default value for a type. To use it, the struct must implement the trait.

Following is a sample program on a struct that implements the Default trait:

```
use std::default::Default;

#[derive(Default)]
struct Point {
    x: i32,
    y: i32,
}
```

With the #[derive(Default)] attribute, Rust will automatically generate an implementation of the Default trait for the Point struct.
You can then use the Default trait to initialize an array of Point structs with default values:

```
let points: [Point; 5] = Default::default();
```

This will create an array of Point structs with all fields set to their default values. In this case, since both x and y are of type i32, their default values will be 0.

Initializing Using Loop and Trait

You can also use a combination of the Default trait and a loop to initialize an array of structs with non-default values:

```rust
let mut points: [Point; 5] = Default::default();

for i in 0..5 {
    points[i] = Point { x: i, y: i * 2 };
}
```

This will create an array of Point structs with the x field set to the loop variable i and the y field set to i * 2.

Recipe#7: Cloning Structs

What Is Cloning of Structs?

In Rust, you can create a copy of a struct by using the clone() method. This is known as cloning the struct.

There are several reasons why you might want to clone a struct:
- You want to create a copy of a struct to use in a different part of your code without modifying the original.
- You want to create a copy of a struct to pass to a function or method as an argument.
- You want to create a copy of a struct to store in a data structure, such as a vector or a hash map.
- To clone a struct, the struct must implement the Clone trait. This is a built-in Rust trait that provides the clone() method.

Implement Clone Trait for Struct

Following is a sample program on a struct that implements the Clone trait:

```rust
#[derive(Clone)]
struct Point {
    x: i32,
    y: i32,
}
```

With the #[derive(Clone)] attribute, Rust will automatically generate an implementation of the Clone trait for the Point struct.

You can then use the clone() method to create a copy of a struct:

```rust
let p1 = Point { x: 1, y: 2 };
let p2 = p1.clone();
```

In this example, we create a Point struct named p1 with the fields x and y set to 1 and 2, respectively. We then create a copy of p1 and store it in a new Point struct named p2.

You can also use the clone() method to clone an array of structs:

```rust
let points: [Point; 5] = [
    Point { x: 0, y: 0 },
    Point { x: 1, y: 0 },
    Point { x: 2, y: 0 },
    Point { x: 3, y: 0 },
    Point { x: 4, y: 0 },
];

let cloned_points = points.clone();
```

This will create a new array named cloned_points that is a copy of the original points array.

CHAPTER 3: PATTERN MATCHING, CONCURRENCY, POINTERS AND MODULES

Recipe#1: Pattern Matching with Enum

Need of Pattern Matching with Enum

Enum types in Rust are used to represent a fixed set of values, which makes them useful for a variety of purposes. One common use of enums is to define a set of possible values that a piece of code can take on, and then use pattern matching to determine the correct behavior based on the value of the enum.

Pattern matching allows you to specify a set of patterns to match against an expression, and then specify code to execute based on which pattern matches. This is particularly useful with enums because it allows you to handle each of the possible values of the enum in a concise and flexible way.

For example, consider the following enum and pattern matching code in Rust:

```rust
enum Direction {
    North,
    South,
    East,
    West,
}

fn move_in_direction(dir: Direction) {
    match dir {
        Direction::North => println!("Moving north"),
        Direction::South => println!("Moving south"),
        Direction::East => println!("Moving east"),
        Direction::West => println!("Moving west"),
    }
}
```

In this example, the Direction enum represents the four cardinal directions, and the move_in_direction function takes a Direction as an argument. The function uses pattern matching to determine which message to print based on the value of the Direction enum.

Overall, pattern matching with enums is useful because it allows you to handle each possible value of an enum in a concise and flexible way, making it easier to write code that can handle a wide range of inputs.

Implement Pattern Matching In Rust Applications

Following code guides how to use pattern matching with enums in any Rust application:

```rust
enum Direction {
    North,
    South,
    East,
    West,
}

struct Point {
    x: i32,
    y: i32,
}

fn move_point(point: &mut Point, dir: Direction) {
    match dir {
        Direction::North => point.y += 1,
        Direction::South => point.y -= 1,
        Direction::East => point.x += 1,
        Direction::West => point.x -= 1,
    }
}
```

```rust
fn main() {
    let mut point = Point { x: 0, y: 0 };
    move_point(&mut point, Direction::North);
    println!("Moved to ({}, {})", point.x, point.y);
}
```

In this example, we have an enum called Direction that represents the four cardinal directions, and a struct called Point that represents a point on a 2D grid. We also have a function called move_point that takes a mutable reference to a Point and a Direction, and moves the point in the specified direction.

The move_point function uses pattern matching to determine which direction to move the point based on the value of the Direction enum. In the main function, we create a new Point at the origin (0, 0), and then use the move_point function to move it one unit north.

Finally, we print the new coordinates of the point to the console to show that it has been moved. When run, this program will output "Moved to (0, 1)".

Recipe#2: Working with Tokio

Basics About Tokio

Tokio is an open source Rust library for building asynchronous, scalable network applications. It is designed to be used with the Rust async/await syntax, which makes it easier to write asynchronous code that is easy to read and understand.

Tokio provides a number of tools and abstractions for building network applications, including:
- A multi-threaded, async-aware runtime for executing async tasks
- Abstractions for working with TCP and UDP sockets

- Tools for building servers and clients using the HTTP and WebSocket protocols
- Utilities for working with timers and timeouts

By using Tokio, you can write asynchronous network applications in Rust that are efficient and easy to reason about. It is a popular choice for building high-performance network servers and clients in Rust.

Installing and Configuring Tokio

To install and use Tokio in a Rust project, you will need to add it as a dependency in your Cargo.toml file:

```
[dependencies]
tokio = { version = "0.3", features = ["full"] }
```

Then, in your Rust code, you can use use tokio::prelude::* to import the Tokio prelude, which provides a number of useful functions and types for working with Tokio.

Following is a sample program on how you might use Tokio to build a simple TCP server in Rust:

```
use tokio::prelude::*;
use tokio::net::TcpListener;

#[tokio::main]
async fn main() -> Result<(), Box<dyn std::error::Error>> {
    let mut listener =
TcpListener::bind("127.0.0.1:8080").await?;

    loop {
        let (mut socket, _) = listener.accept().await?;

        tokio::spawn(async move {
```

```
        let mut buf = [0; 1024];

        // Read data from the socket
        let n = socket.read(&mut buf).await.unwrap();

        // Write the data back to the socket
        socket.write_all(&buf[0..n]).await.unwrap();
    });
    }
}
```

This code creates a TCP listener that listens for incoming connections on port 8080, and then spawns a new async task to handle each incoming connection. The task reads data from the socket, and then writes it back to the socket.

Recipe#3: Writing Concurrent Programming

What Is Concurrency In Rust?

Concurrency is the ability of a program to execute multiple tasks simultaneously. Rust provides a number of tools and features for building concurrent programs, including:

- Threads: Rust's std::thread module provides a way to create and manage native threads. Threads allow you to parallelize your code by running multiple tasks concurrently on different CPU cores.

- Async/await: Rust's async/await syntax provides a way to write asynchronous code that is easy to read and understand. Async functions can be awaited to pause their execution until a value becomes available, allowing multiple async tasks to be run concurrently.

- Channels: Rust's std::sync::mpsc module provides channels, which are a way to send messages between threads. Channels allow you to safely communicate between threads without using locks or other synchronization primitives.

- Atomic variables: Rust's std::sync::atomic module provides atomic variables, which are variables that can be accessed and modified concurrently from multiple threads without the need for locks.

By using these tools and features, you can build concurrent programs in Rust that are efficient, safe, and easy to reason about. It is important to note that concurrent programming can be challenging, and it is important to carefully design and test concurrent programs to ensure that they are correct and free of race conditions and other concurrency bugs.

Procedure to Build Concurrent Programs

Following are some helpful general steps you can follow to build a concurrent program in Rust:
- Identify the tasks that you want to run concurrently. These tasks might be independent of each other, or they might need to communicate and coordinate with each other in some way.
- Decide on the concurrency model you want to use. Depending on your needs, you might use threads, async/await, or some combination of both.
- Design the communication and coordination between tasks. If your tasks need to communicate with each other, you will need to decide on the appropriate communication mechanism. Options include channels, shared variables, and message passing.
- Implement the concurrent tasks. Use Rust's concurrency tools and features to implement the tasks and the communication and coordination between them.
- Test and debug your concurrent program. Concurrent programs can be difficult to test and debug due to the potential for race conditions and other concurrency bugs. It is important to carefully test and debug your concurrent program to ensure that it is correct and free of concurrency issues.

Overall, building a concurrent program in Rust involves designing and implementing the tasks and communication between them, and then testing and debugging the program to ensure that it is correct and free of concurrency issues. It can be a challenging process, but Rust provides a number of tools and features to make it easier to build concurrent programs that are efficient, safe, and easy to reason about.

Implementing Concurrency to Existing Applications

Following is an example of a concurrent program in Rust that uses async/await to perform multiple tasks concurrently:

```rust
use std::time::Duration;
use tokio::time::delay_for;
use tokio::sync::mpsc;

async fn task1() {
    println!("Task 1 started");
    delay_for(Duration::from_secs(2)).await;
    println!("Task 1 finished");
}

async fn task2() {
    println!("Task 2 started");
    delay_for(Duration::from_secs(1)).await;
    println!("Task 2 finished");
}

async fn run_tasks() {
    let mut tasks = vec![task1(), task2()];
    while let Some(mut task) = tasks.pop() {
        task.await;
    }
}

#[tokio::main]
async fn main() {
    run_tasks().await;
}
```

In this example, we have two async tasks called task1 and task2 that each perform some work and then delay for a set amount of time. We then have an async function called run_tasks that executes both tasks concurrently by using the await keyword.

Finally, we use the tokio::main attribute to indicate that the main function is an async function, and then we use await to run the run_tasks function. When this program is run, the tasks will be executed concurrently, and the output will be:

```
Task 1 started
Task 2 started
Task 2 finished
Task 1 finished
```

This example demonstrates how you can use async/await in Rust to perform multiple tasks concurrently. It is a simple example, but it illustrates the basic concepts of concurrent programming in Rust using async/await.

Recipe#4: Working with Raw Pointers

Why Raw Pointers?

In Rust, a raw pointer is a type of pointer that does not have any associated safety guarantees. Raw pointers are represented by the *const T and *mut T types, where T is the type of the value being pointed to.

Raw pointers are useful in situations where you need to interface with foreign code or legacy systems that do not use Rust's borrowing and ownership rules. They are also useful for certain low-level tasks such as implementing data structures or working with hardware.

However, raw pointers come with some risks. They do not have any of the safety guarantees provided by Rust's borrow checker, so it is easy to create dangling pointers or cause memory safety issues if you are not careful. Therefore, it is generally recommended to use safer pointer types such as references (&T) or smart pointers (e.g. Box<T>, Rc<T>) whenever possible.

How to Use Raw Pointers In Rust Applications?

Following is a sample program on how you might use raw pointers in Rust:

```rust
let x = 10;
let y = 20;

let mut p: *mut i32 = &mut x;
unsafe {
    *p = y;
}

assert_eq!(x, 20);
```

In this example, we have two integers x and y, and we create a raw mutable pointer p to x. We then use the unsafe block to dereference the pointer and modify the value of x through the pointer. After the unsafe block, we can see that the value of x has been changed to 20.

It is important to note that using raw pointers requires using the unsafe keyword, which indicates that the code is potentially unsafe and requires special handling by the Rust compiler. Code inside an unsafe block is not checked by the borrow checker or other safety checks, so it is important to use caution when working with raw pointers.

Use of Multiple Raw Pointers

Using multiple raw pointers in Rust can be useful in certain situations, such as when working with foreign code or legacy systems that do not use Rust's borrowing and ownership rules. However, it is important to be careful when working with multiple raw pointers, as it can be easy to create dangling pointers or cause memory safety issues if you are not careful.

Following is a sample program on how you might use multiple raw pointers in Rust:

```rust
let x = 10;
let y = 20;

let p: *mut i32 = &mut x;
let q: *mut i32 = &mut y;

unsafe {
    *p = *q;
}

assert_eq!(x, 20);
```

In this example, we have two integers x and y, and we create two raw mutable pointers p and q to x and y, respectively. We then use an unsafe block to dereference both pointers and copy the value of y into x through the pointers. After the unsafe block, we can see that the value of x has been changed to 20.

If you need to work with multiple raw pointers, it is important to ensure that you are correctly handling ownership and memory safety. This might involve using proper synchronization mechanisms such as mutexes or atomic variables to protect shared data, and carefully managing the lifetime of the pointers to ensure that they do not become dangling.

Recipe#5: Working with Smart Pointers

Understanding Smart Pointers

Smart pointers are a type of pointer that provides additional functionality beyond simply pointing to a value. They are commonly used in Rust to manage the lifetime of values, particularly in situations where it is not convenient or possible to use Rust's borrowing and ownership rules.

There are several types of smart pointers available in Rust, including:

- Box<T>: A smart pointer that owns a value and frees it when it goes out of scope. Box<T> is useful for allocating values on the heap and owning them.
- Rc<T>: A reference-counted smart pointer that allows multiple owners of a value. Rc<T> is useful for sharing values between multiple owners in a thread-safe manner.
- Arc<T>: A multi-threaded version of Rc<T>, which allows multiple owners of a value in different threads. Arc<T> is useful for sharing values between multiple owners in a concurrent environment.
- Weak<T>: A non-owning version of Rc<T>, which allows multiple owners of a value but does not increment the reference count. Weak<T> is useful for creating cyclic data structures or breaking reference cycles.

Smart pointers are often used in Rust to manage the lifetime of values and to share values between multiple owners in a safe and convenient way. They are particularly useful when working with complex data structures or in situations where it is not possible or convenient to use Rust's borrowing and ownership rules.

Following is a sample program on how you might use the Box<T> smart pointer in Rust:

```rust
fn main() {
    let x = 10;
    let y = Box::new(20);

    println!("x = {}", x);
    println!("y = {}", *y);
}
```

In this example, we have two values x and y. x is a regular integer, while y is a Box<i32> that owns an integer value on the heap. We can access the value of y through the Box by dereferencing it with the * operator. When this code is run, it will print "x = 10" and "y = 20".

Overall, smart pointers are a useful tool in Rust for managing the lifetime of values and for sharing values between multiple owners in a safe and convenient way. They are particularly useful in complex data structures and in situations where it is not possible or convenient to use Rust's borrowing and ownership rules.

Smart Pointers Vs Raw Pointers?

Smart pointers and raw pointers are both types of pointers in Rust, but they have some important differences:

- Safety: Smart pointers provide additional safety guarantees that raw pointers do not. For example, Box<T> automatically deallocates the memory it points to when it goes out of scope, while Rc<T> and Arc<T> provide thread-safe reference counting. Raw pointers, on the other hand, do not have any of these safety guarantees, and it is easy to create dangling pointers or cause memory safety issues if you are not careful.
- Ownership: Smart pointers typically have ownership of the values they point to, while raw pointers do not. This means that when a smart pointer goes out of scope, the value it points to is automatically deallocated or dropped, while raw pointers do not have this behavior.
- Syntax: Smart pointers use a different syntax than raw pointers. For example, Box<T> is written as Box<T>, while raw pointers are written as *const T or *mut T.

Overall, smart pointers are generally safer and easier to use than raw pointers, as they provide additional safety guarantees and have a more convenient syntax. However, raw pointers can be useful in certain situations, such as when working with foreign code or legacy systems that do not use Rust's borrowing and ownership rules, or for certain low-level tasks such as implementing data structures or working with hardware. It is important to carefully consider the trade-offs between safety and flexibility when deciding which type of pointer to use in your code.

How to Implement Smart Pointer In a Rust Program

Following is a sample program on how you might use the Rc<T> smart pointer in a Rust program:

```rust
use std::rc::Rc;

struct Node {
    value: i32,
    next: Option<Rc<Node>>,
}

fn main() {
    let a = Rc::new(Node {
        value: 10,
        next: None,
    });
    let b = Rc::new(Node {
        value: 20,
        next: Some(a.clone()),
    });
    let c = Rc::new(Node {
        value: 30,
        next: Some(a.clone()),
    });

    println!("a = {:?}", a);
    println!("b = {:?}", b);
    println!("c = {:?}", c);
}
```

value and a reference to the next node in the list. The next field is an Option<Rc<Node>>, which means that it is either None or a reference-counted pointer to a Node.

We then create three nodes a, b, and c, and set the next field of b and c to a. We do this by using the Rc::clone method to create a new reference to a. This increments the reference count of a, ensuring that it is not dropped until all the references to it go out of scope.

Finally, we print out the nodes using the Debug trait. When this code is run, it will print something like:

In this example, we have a simple linked list data structure with Node structs that contain an integer

```
a = Node { value: 10, next: None }
b = Node { value: 20, next: Some(Node { value: 10, next: None
}) }
c = Node { value: 30, next: Some(Node { value: 10, next: None
}) }
```

This example demonstrates how you can use the Rc<T> smart pointer to create a simple linked list data structure in Rust. It illustrates how Rc<T> can be used to create multiple owners of a value and how the reference count is automatically managed to ensure that the value is not dropped until all the references to it go out of scope.

Using smart pointers like Rc<T> can be particularly useful in Rust when working with complex data structures or in situations where it is not convenient or possible to use Rust's borrowing and ownership rules. In this case, the Rc<T> smart pointer allows us to create a linked list data structure with multiple owners of each node, without having to worry about manually managing the lifetime of the nodes or the references between them.

However, it is important to be aware that using Rc<T> (or any reference-counted smart pointer) can have some performance overhead compared to using raw pointers or other smart pointers, as it requires additional atomic operations to maintain the reference count. Therefore, it is important to carefully consider the trade-offs between performance and convenience when deciding which type of pointer to use in your code.

Recipe#6: Using 'mod' Modules

Declaring Mod

In Rust, the mod keyword is used to define and declare modules. A module is a named unit of Rust code that can contain other items such as functions, structs, enums, and other modules. Modules can be organized into a tree-like structure to help organize and reuse code.

Following is a sample program on how you might define and declare a module in Rust:

```rust
mod my_module {
    fn my_function() {
        // function body goes here
    }

    struct MyStruct {
        // struct fields go here
    }

    impl MyStruct {
        fn new() -> MyStruct {
            // implementation goes here
        }
    }
}
```

In this example, we define a module called my_module that contains a function my_function, a struct MyStruct, and an implementation of MyStruct. The items inside the module are private by default, meaning that they can only be accessed from within the module or by other items that have been granted explicit access through the pub keyword.

To use items from a module in your code, you can either use the use keyword to bring them into scope, or you can use the fully qualified path to the item. For example:

```
use my_module::MyStruct;

let s = MyStruct::new();

// or

let t = my_module::MyStruct::new();
```

Overall, modules are a powerful tool in Rust for organizing and reusing code, and they can help you create clean and maintainable codebases.

Advantages of Using Mod

Using the mod keyword in an existing Rust program can have a number of effects, depending on how the module is defined and used.

One common use of modules in Rust is to organize code into logical units and to reuse code across multiple parts of a program. For example, you might define a module for common utility functions that are used throughout your program, or for a group of related structs and enums. By organizing your code into modules, you can make your codebase more readable and maintainable, and you can avoid name clashes between items with the same name.

Another use of modules in Rust is to control the visibility of items in your code. By default, items inside a module are private, meaning that they can only be accessed from within the module or by other items that have been granted explicit access through the pub keyword. This can be useful for creating a clear separation between the public API of your code and the internal implementation details.

Using modules can also have performance implications in Rust, depending on how the module is defined and used. For example, using mod to define inline modules (i.e. modules defined within the same file as the parent module) can improve compile times and binary size, as the compiler can optimize the code more aggressively. On the other hand, using mod to define external modules (i.e.

modules defined in a separate file) can have a negative impact on compile times, as the compiler has to read and parse the additional files.

Overall, using the mod keyword in an existing Rust program can have a number of effects, including improving code organization and reuse, controlling item visibility, and potentially impacting performance. It is important to carefully consider the trade-offs between these effects when deciding whether and how to use modules in your code.

Implement Mod In Existing Rust Program?

To implement a module in a Rust program, you can use the mod keyword followed by the name of the module. The module definition goes inside a pair of curly braces {}, and it can contain other items such as functions, structs, enums, and other modules.

Following is a sample program on how you might implement a module in a Rust program:

```rust
mod my_module {
    fn my_function() {
        // function body goes here
    }

    struct MyStruct {
        // struct fields go here
    }

    impl MyStruct {
        fn new() -> MyStruct {
            // implementation goes here
        }
    }
}

fn main() {
```

```
    // use items from my_module here
}
```

In this example, we define a module called my_module that contains a function my_function, a struct MyStruct, and an implementation of MyStruct. The items inside the module are private by default, meaning that they can only be accessed from within the module or by other items that have been granted explicit access through the pub keyword.

To use items from the module in your code, you can either use the use keyword to bring them into scope, or you can use the fully qualified path to the item. For example:

```
use my_module::MyStruct;

let s = MyStruct::new();

// or

let t = my_module::MyStruct::new();
```

CHAPTER 4: USING DECLARATIVE AND PROCEDURAL MACROS

Recipe#1: Declaring and Implementing Declarative Macros

Defining Declarative Macros

Declarative macros in Rust are a way to define custom syntax for your program. They allow you to define a macro that can be invoked in your code with a specific pattern, and the macro will expand to a block of code that you define.

Declarative macros are defined using the macro_rules! macro. Following is a sample program on how to define a simple declarative macro called say_hello:

```rust
macro_rules! say_hello {
    () => {
        println!("Hello, world!");
    };
}
```

To invoke this macro, you can use the macro name followed by a set of parentheses, like this:

```rust
say_hello!();
```

This will expand to the code block defined in the macro, which will print "Hello, world!" to the console.

Declarative macros can also take arguments. For example, you can define a macro that takes a name and prints a personalized greeting:

```rust
macro_rules! greet {
```

```
    ($name:expr) => {
        println!("Hello, {}!", $name);
    };
}
```

To invoke this macro, you can pass an argument within the parentheses, like this:

```
greet!("Alice");
```

This will expand to the code block defined in the macro, which will print "Hello, Alice!" to the console.

Declarative macros can be very powerful, but they can also be complex to define and use. They are most commonly used for code generation, where you want to generate a large block of code based on a set of inputs.

Creating Declarative Macro

Following is an example of how to create a declarative macro in Rust:

```
macro_rules! create_function {
    // This macro takes an argument of type `ident` (an
identifier) and
    // creates a function named after that identifier.
    ($func_name:ident) => {
        fn $func_name() {
            // The macro will expand to a function
definition, using the
            // identifier passed as an argument as the
function name.
            println!("You called the function named {}",
stringify!($func_name));
```

```rust
        }
    };
}

// Now we can use the macro to create a function.
create_function!(foo);

// This will expand to a function definition:
// fn foo() {
//          println!("You  called  the  function  named  {}",
stringify!(foo));
// }

fn main() {
    // We can now call the function we created with the macro.
    foo();
}
```

In this example, we define a macro called create_function that takes an identifier as an argument and creates a function with that name. We can then use the macro to create a function named foo.

The macro is invoked using the macro name followed by an exclamation point and a set of parentheses containing the argument. In this case, we pass the identifier foo as an argument to the macro.

The macro expands to a function definition, using the identifier passed as an argument as the function name. In this case, the macro expands to a function definition for a function named foo.

We can then call the function in the same way as any other function. In this example, we call the foo function in the main function.

Recipe#2: Debugging Declarative Macros

Steps to Debug Declarative Macro

Debugging declarative macros can be challenging, as they involve expanding code at compile time rather than runtime. Here are a few tips that will guided you to run debugging to a good extent:

- Use the #[macro_export] attribute to make your macro available in other modules. This will allow you to test your macro in a separate module, which can make debugging easier.
- Use the #[cfg(test)] attribute to wrap your test cases in a separate module. This will allow you to use the cargo test command to run your tests, which will give you more detailed output when your tests fail.
- Use the println! macro to print out intermediate values in your macro code. This can help you understand what's going wrong and where.
- Use the stringify! macro to print out the source code of your macro arguments. This can help you understand what your macro is receiving as input and how it is being processed.
- Use the rustc command-line tool to see the intermediate representation (IR) of your macro code. This can help you understand how your macro is being expanded and can give you a more detailed view of what's going wrong.

How to Debug Series of Declarative Macros In Rust Programs

To debug the declarative macro that we defined in the previous example, you can use some of the techniques I mentioned earlier:

- Use the #[macro_export] attribute to make your macro available in other modules. This will allow you to test your macro in a separate module, which can make debugging easier.

For example, you can add the #[macro_export] attribute to your macro definition like this:

```
#[macro_export]
macro_rules! create_function {
```

```
    // ...
}
```

Then, you can create a separate module in your project and import the macro using the use keyword:

```
use crate::create_function;

#[cfg(test)]
mod tests {
    #[test]
    fn test_create_function() {
        // Test the create_function macro here
    }
}
```

- Use the #[cfg(test)] attribute to wrap your test cases in a separate module. This will allow you to use the cargo test command to run your tests, which will give you more detailed output when your tests fail.

For example, you can create a separate module for your tests and use the #[cfg(test)] attribute to wrap your test cases like this:

```
#[cfg(test)]
mod tests {
    #[test]
    fn test_create_function() {
        // Test the create_function macro here
    }
}
```

Then, you can run your tests using the cargo test command.

- Use the println! macro to print out intermediate values in your macro code. This can help you understand what's going wrong and where.

For example, you can add println! statements to your macro code to print out the values of intermediate variables:

```
macro_rules! create_function {
    ($func_name:ident) => {
        fn $func_name() {
            println!("func_name                     =                     {}",
stringify!($func_name));
            println!("You   called   the   function   named   {}",
stringify!($func_name));
        }
    };
}
```

This will print out the values of func_name and $func_name at runtime, which can help you understand how your macro is being expanded.

- Use the stringify! macro to print out the source code of your macro arguments. This can help you understand what your macro is receiving as input and how it is being processed.

For example, you can use the stringify! macro to print out the source code of your macro arguments like this:

```
macro_rules! create_function {
    ($func_name:ident) => {
        fn $func_name() {
            println!("func_name                     =                     {}",
stringify!($func_name));
            println!("You   called   the   function   named   {}",
stringify!($func_name));
```

```
        }
    };
}
```

This will print out the source code of $func_name, which can help you understand how your macro is being expanded.

Recipe#3: Using Derive Macro for Implementing Traits

Understanding Derive Macro As An Procedural Macro

Derive macros in Rust allow you to automatically implement certain traits for your types using the #[derive] attribute. This can save you a lot of boilerplate code and make it easier to write correct, efficient code.

Derive macros can be very powerful, but they can also be complex to define and use. They are most commonly used for automatically implementing traits that would otherwise require a lot of boilerplate code to implement manually.

To implement a derive macro, you'll need to use the proc_macro_derive crate.

Implementing Derive Macros

Following is a sample program on how to define a simple derive macro that implements the Debug trait for a struct:

```
extern crate proc_macro;
```

```rust
use proc_macro::TokenStream;
use quote::quote;
use syn::{parse_macro_input, DeriveInput};

#[proc_macro_derive(Debug)]
pub fn debug_derive(input: TokenStream) -> TokenStream {
    // Parse the input tokens into a syntax tree
    let ast: DeriveInput = parse_macro_input!(input);

    // Build the output tokens
    let expanded = quote! {
        impl ::std::fmt::Debug for #ast {
            fn fmt(&self, f: &mut ::std::fmt::Formatter) ->
::std::fmt::Result {
                // Define the formatting for the struct
                let             mut             f             =
f.debug_struct(stringify!(#ast));

                // Add each field to the output
                #(f.field(stringify!(#ast.#ast_field_name),
&self.#ast_field_name);)*

                // Finish the output and return it
                f.finish()
            }
        }
    };

    // Return the expanded tokens
    TokenStream::from(expanded)
}
```

To use this derive macro, you can add the #[derive(Debug)] attribute to your struct definition:

```rust
#[derive(Debug)]
struct MyStruct {
    field1: i32,
    field2: String,
}
```

Recipe#4: Using Function-Like Macros

Understanding Function-Like Macros

Function-like macros in Rust are a way to define custom syntax for your program that looks like a function call. They allow you to define a macro that can be invoked in your code with a specific pattern, and the macro will expand to a block of code that you define.

Function-like macros are defined using the macro_rules! macro, just like declarative macros. However, they are invoked using the ident!(...) syntax, where ident is the name of the macro and ... are the arguments passed to the macro.

Function-like macros can be very powerful, but they can also be complex to define and use. They are most commonly used for code generation, where you want to generate a large block of code based on a set of inputs.

Implementing Function-Like Macro

Following is a sample program on how to define a simple function-like macro called add_one:

```rust
macro_rules! add_one {
    // This macro takes an argument of type `expr` (an
```

```
expression) and
    // adds 1 to it.
    ($x:expr) => {
        $x + 1
    };
}
```

To invoke this macro, you can use the macro name followed by an exclamation point and a set of parentheses containing the argument, like this:

```
let x = add_one!(5);
```

This will expand to the code block defined in the macro, which will add 1 to the value of 5 and assign the result to x.

Function-like macros can also take multiple arguments and return a value. For example, you can define a macro that takes two numbers and returns their sum:

```
macro_rules! add {
    ($x:expr, $y:expr) => {
        $x + $y
    };
}
```

To invoke this macro, you can pass two arguments within the parentheses, like this:

```
let sum = add!(5, 10);
```

This will expand to the code block defined in the macro, which will add the values of 5 and 10 and assign the result to sum.

Recipe#5: Using Attribute Macros

Understanding Attribute Macros

Attribute macros in Rust are a way to define custom syntax for your program that looks like an attribute. They allow you to define a macro that can be invoked in your code by adding an attribute to a item, and the macro will expand to a block of code that you define.

Attribute macros can be very powerful, but they can also be complex to define and use. They are most commonly used for code generation, where you want to generate a large block of code based on a set of inputs.

Implementing Attribute Macro

Attribute macros are defined using the #[proc_macro_attribute] attribute. Following is a sample program on how to define a simple attribute macro called say_hello:

```rust
use proc_macro::TokenStream;

#[proc_macro_attribute]
pub fn say_hello(_attr: TokenStream, item: TokenStream) ->
TokenStream {
    // The `say_hello` attribute can be applied to any item
(e.g. a function, struct, etc.)
    // The `item` argument is the token stream representing
the item being decorated

    // Define the code to insert before the item
    let prefix = "println!(\"Hello, world!\");\n";

    // Convert the prefix code to a token stream
    let                       prefix_tokens                 =
```

```
proc_macro2::TokenStream::from_str(prefix).unwrap();

    // Concatenate the prefix tokens and the item tokens
    let     expanded    =     quote::format_ident!("{}     {}",
prefix_tokens, item);

    // Return the expanded token stream
    TokenStream::from(expanded)
}
```

To use this attribute macro, you can add the #[say_hello] attribute to any item in your code:

```
#[say_hello]
fn foo() {
    // This function will have the code "println!("Hello,
world!");" inserted before it
    // when the attribute macro is expanded.
}
```

Recipe#6: Debugging Procedural Macros

Tips and Tricks to Debug Procedural Macros

Debugging procedural macros can be challenging, as they involve expanding code at compile time rather than runtime. Here are a few tips that might help:

- Use the println! macro to print out intermediate values in your macro code. This can help you understand what's going wrong and where.
- Use the stringify! macro to print out the source code of your macro arguments. This can help you understand what your macro is receiving as input and how it is being processed.
- Use the quote! macro to print out the intermediate representation (IR) of your macro code.

This can help you understand how your macro is being expanded and can give you a more detailed view of what's going wrong.

- Use the rustc command-line tool to see the intermediate representation (IR) of your macro code. This can help you understand how your macro is being expanded and can give you a more detailed view of what's going wrong.

- Use the #[cfg(test)] attribute to wrap your test cases in a separate module. This will allow you to use the cargo test command to run your tests, which will give you more detailed output when your tests fail.

- Use the #[macro_export] attribute to make your macro available in other modules. This will allow you to test your macro in a separate module, which can make debugging easier.

Techniques of Debugging

Following is a sample program of procedural macro that uses these techniques to debug a problem:

```rust
#[proc_macro]
pub fn debug_macro(input: TokenStream) -> TokenStream {
    // Parse the input tokens into a syntax tree.
    let input = parse_macro_input!(input as ItemFn);

    // Print some debug messages.
    #[cfg(debug_assertions)]
    println!("input: {:?}", input);

    // Check for a specific condition and panic if it occurs.
    let ident = input.sig.ident.to_string();
    if ident.starts_with("foo") {
        panic!("function names starting with 'foo' are not allowed");
    }
```

```rust
    // Return the modified syntax tree as tokens.
    TokenStream::from(quote! {
        #input
    })
}
```

In this example, the debug_macro procedural macro parses the input tokens into a syntax tree, and then uses the #[cfg(debug_assertions)] attribute to print some debug messages and the panic! macro to raise an error if a specific condition is met.

CHAPTER 5:
IMPLEMENTING CONCURRENCY AND MULTITHREADING

Concurrency in Rust refers to the ability of a program to execute multiple tasks concurrently. This means that the program can perform multiple tasks at the same time, rather than waiting for one task to complete before starting the next one.

Multithreading in Rust refers to the ability of a program to execute multiple threads concurrently. A thread is a separate execution context within a program, and each thread can run concurrently with the other threads in the program.

Using concurrency and multithreading can greatly improve the performance and responsiveness of a program, as it allows the program to take full advantage of modern multi-core processors. However, it also introduces a number of challenges for developers.

One major challenge is the need to manage shared data access. When multiple threads are running concurrently, they may need to access shared data, and it's important to ensure that they do so in a way that is safe and doesn't result in race conditions or data corruption. Rust provides a number of tools to help with this, including mutexes and atomic variables, but it's still up to the developer to use these tools correctly.

Another challenge is the need to manage the lifecycle of threads. When creating a new thread, it's important to ensure that the thread is terminated properly when it's no longer needed, and that any resources it uses are cleaned up correctly. Rust provides a number of tools to help with this, including the join method and the Arc and Rc types, but it's still up to the developer to use these tools correctly.

Finally, it's important to ensure that concurrent programs are correct and maintainable. This can be challenging because concurrent programs can be difficult to reason about, and it's easy to introduce bugs or make the code hard to understand. Rust provides a number of tools to help with this, including the std::sync::Mutex type and the Arc and Rc types, but it's still up to the developer to use these tools correctly.

Recipe#1: Implementing Concurrent Threadsafe Queues

Rust provides a number of ways to implement concurrent threadsafe queues, each with their own trade-offs in terms of performance, complexity, and level of control. Here are three common options:

Using Arc<Mutex<T>>

Arc<Mutex<T>>: This is a simple and convenient way to implement a concurrent threadsafe queue using Rust's built-in synchronization primitives. An Arc (atomic reference count) is used to enable multiple threads to have shared access to the queue, and a Mutex (mutual exclusion lock) is used to ensure that only one thread can modify the queue at a time.

Following is a sample program on on how you might implement a simple concurrent queue using this approach:

```rust
use std::sync::{Arc, Mutex};

struct ConcurrentQueue<T> {
    inner: Arc<Mutex<Vec<T>>>,
}

impl<T> ConcurrentQueue<T> {
    fn new() -> Self {
        ConcurrentQueue {
            inner: Arc::new(Mutex::new(Vec::new())),
        }
    }

    fn push(&self, value: T) {
```

```rust
        let mut inner = self.inner.lock().unwrap();
        inner.push(value);
    }

    fn pop(&self) -> Option<T> {
        let mut inner = self.inner.lock().unwrap();
        inner.pop()
    }
}
```

Using Std::Sync::Mpsc::Channel()

std::sync::mpsc::channel(): This method creates a multi-producer, single-consumer (MPSC) channel, which allows multiple threads to send values to a single thread, and is often used to implement concurrent queues.

Following is a sample program on how you might use a channel to implement a concurrent queue:

```rust
use std::sync::mpsc::{channel, Receiver, Sender};

struct ConcurrentQueue<T> {
    sender: Sender<T>,
    receiver: Receiver<T>,
}

impl<T> ConcurrentQueue<T> {
    fn new() -> (Self, Receiver<T>) {
        let (sender, receiver) = channel();
        (ConcurrentQueue { sender, receiver }, receiver)
    }

    fn push(&self, value: T) {
        self.sender.send(value).unwrap();
```

```
        }
}
```

Using Crossbeam::Channel::Bounded()

crossbeam::channel::bounded(): This method creates a bounded MPSC channel, which allows you to set a maximum capacity for the queue. This can be useful if you want to limit the amount of memory used by the queue, or if you want to implement a form of backpressure to prevent producer threads from overloading the consumer.

Following is a sample program on how you might use a bounded channel to implement a concurrent queue:

```
use crossbeam::channel::{bounded, Receiver, Sender};

struct ConcurrentQueue<T> {
    sender: Sender<T>,
    receiver: Receiver<T>,
}

impl<T> ConcurrentQueue<T> {
    fn new(capacity: usize) -> (Self, Receiver<T>) {
        let (sender, receiver) = bounded(capacity);
        (ConcurrentQueue { sender, receiver }, receiver)
    }

    fn push(&self, value: T) {
        self.sender.send(value).unwrap();
    }
}
```

Recipe#2: Implementing Concurrent Hash Maps

Understanding Concurrent Hash Map

A concurrent hash map is a data structure that allows multiple threads to access and modify the map concurrently, without the need for explicit synchronization. There are several ways to implement a concurrent hash map in Rust, each with their own trade-offs in terms of performance, complexity, and level of control. Here are two common options:

Arc<Mutex<Hashmap<K, V>>> for Concurrent Hash Map

Arc<Mutex<HashMap<K, V>>>: This is a simple and convenient way to implement a concurrent hash map using Rust's built-in synchronization primitives. An Arc (atomic reference count) is used to enable multiple threads to have shared access to the map, and a Mutex (mutual exclusion lock) is used to ensure that only one thread can modify the map at a time.

Following is a sample program on how you might implement a simple concurrent hash map using this approach:

```rust
use std::collections::HashMap;
use std::sync::{Arc, Mutex};

struct ConcurrentHashMap<K, V> {
    inner: Arc<Mutex<HashMap<K, V>>>,
}

impl<K, V> ConcurrentHashMap<K, V>
where
    K: std::cmp::Eq + std::hash::Hash + Send + 'static,
    V: Send + 'static,
{
```

```rust
    fn new() -> Self {
        ConcurrentHashMap {
            inner: Arc::new(Mutex::new(HashMap::new())),
        }
    }

    fn insert(&self, key: K, value: V) {
        let mut inner = self.inner.lock().unwrap();
        inner.insert(key, value);
    }

    fn get(&self, key: &K) -> Option<V> {
        let inner = self.inner.lock().unwrap();
        inner.get(key).cloned()
    }
}

fn main() {
    let map = ConcurrentHashMap::new();

    // Spawn some threads that concurrently insert and get
values from the map.
    for i in 0..10 {
        let map = map.clone();
        std::thread::spawn(move || {
            map.insert(i, i * 2);
            let value = map.get(&i);
            println!("{:?}", value);
        });
    }
}
```

Rayon for Concurrent Hash Map

Rayon: This is a popular crate that provides parallelism and concurrency support, including a concurrent hash map implementation.

Following is a sample program on how you might use the Rayon crate to implement a concurrent hash map:

```rust
use rayon::prelude::*;
use std::collections::HashMap;

struct ConcurrentHashMap<K, V> {
    inner: HashMap<K, V>,
}

impl<K, V> ConcurrentHashMap<K, V>
where
    K: std::cmp::Eq + std::hash::Hash + Send + 'static,
    V: Send + 'static,
{
    fn new() -> Self {
        ConcurrentHashMap {
            inner: HashMap::new(),
        }
    }

    fn insert(&mut self, key: K, value: V) {
        self.inner.insert(key, value);
    }

    fn get(&self, key: &K) -> Option<&V> {
        self.inner.get(key)
    }
}

fn main() {
```

```rust
let mut map = ConcurrentHashMap::new();

// Insert some values into the map.
(0..10).into_par_iter().for_each(|i| {
    map.insert(i, i * 2);
});

// Get the values from the map.
(0..10).into_par_iter().for_each(|i| {
    let value = map.get(&i);
    println!("{:?}", value);
});
}
```

This code creates a new concurrent hash map and then inserts some values into it using parallel iterators from the Rayon crate. It then gets the values from the map using parallel iterators again. The Rayon crate takes care of the underlying concurrency and synchronization details, allowing you to write concurrent code in a simple and easy-to-use way.

Recipe#3: Using Synchronization Mechanisms

Synchronization mechanisms in Rust are used to coordinate access to shared resources between multiple threads, to ensure that the resources are used safely and correctly. There are several synchronization mechanisms available in Rust, including:

Using Mutual Exclusion Lock 'mutex'

Mutex: A mutual exclusion lock (mutex) is used to ensure that only one thread can access a shared resource at a time.

Following is a sample program on how you might use a Mutex to synchronize access to a shared variable:

```rust
use std::sync::Mutex;

fn main() {
    let mutex = Mutex::new(0);

    // Spawn some threads that concurrently increment the
shared variable.
    for _ in 0..10 {
        let mutex = mutex.clone();
        std::thread::spawn(move || {
            let mut value = mutex.lock().unwrap();
            *value += 1;
        });
    }

    // Wait for all the threads to finish.
    let value = mutex.lock().unwrap();
    println!("{}", *value);
}
```

Using Read-Write Lock 'rwlock'

RwLock: A read-write lock (rwlock) is used to allow multiple threads to read a shared resource concurrently, but only allow one thread to write to the resource at a time.

Following is a sample program on how you might use an RwLock to synchronize access to a shared variable:

```rust
use std::sync::RwLock;
```

```rust
fn main() {
    let rwlock = RwLock::new(0);

    // Spawn some threads that concurrently read the shared
variable.
    for _ in 0..10 {
        let rwlock = rwlock.clone();
        std::thread::spawn(move || {
            let value = rwlock.read().unwrap();
            println!("{}", *value);
        });
    }

    // Wait for all the threads to finish.
    let mut value = rwlock.write().unwrap();
    *value += 1;
}
```

Using Atomic

Atomic: An atomic variable is a type of shared variable that provides low-level, lock-free access to a value. Atomic variables are useful for implementing high-performance, concurrent data structures and algorithms.

Following is a sample program on how you might use an Atomic variable to synchronize access to a shared variable:

```rust
use std::sync::atomic::{AtomicUsize, Ordering};

fn main() {
    let atomic = AtomicUsize::new(0);

    // Spawn  some  threads  that  concurrently  increment  the
```

```
shared variable.
    for _ in 0..10 {
        let atomic = atomic.clone();
        std::thread::spawn(move || {
            atomic.fetch_add(1, Ordering::SeqCst);
        });
    }

    // Wait for all the threads to finish.
    let value = atomic.load(Ordering::SeqCst);
    println!("{}", value);
}
```

Recipe#4: Designing Efficient Parallel Algorithms

What are Parallel Algorithms?

Parallel algorithms are algorithms that can be executed concurrently across multiple threads or CPUs, in order to improve performance and efficiency.

Putting Parallel Algorithms Into Use

Rust provides several ways to implement parallel algorithms, including:

- rayon: This is a popular crate that provides parallelism and concurrency support, including a wide range of parallel iterators and other parallel algorithms. Following is a sample program on how you might use the rayon crate to implement a parallel algorithm:

```rust
use rayon::prelude::*;

fn main() {
    // Calculate the sum of the first 100 integers in
parallel.
    let sum: i32 = (1..=100).into_par_iter().sum();
    println!("{}", sum);
}
```

- rayon::join: This is a low-level API that allows you to manually spawn and join threads to implement parallel algorithms. Following is a sample program on how you might use the rayon::join API to implement a parallel algorithm:

```rust
use rayon::join;

fn main() {
    // Calculate the sum of the first 50 integers in one
thread and the sum of the next 50 integers in another thread.
    let (sum1, sum2) = join(|| (1..=50).sum(), ||
(51..=100).sum());
    let sum = sum1 + sum2;
    println!("{}", sum);
}
```

- std::thread: This is the standard library's thread API, which allows you to manually spawn and join threads to implement parallel algorithms. Following is a sample program on how you might use the std::thread API to implement a parallel algorithm:

```rust
use std::thread;

fn main() {
    // Calculate the sum of the first 50 integers in one
thread and the sum of the next 50 integers in another thread.
```

```rust
    let handle1 = thread::spawn(|| (1..=50).sum::<i32>());
    let handle2 = thread::spawn(|| (51..=100).sum::<i32>());
    let sum1 = handle1.join().unwrap();
    let sum2 = handle2.join().unwrap();
    let sum = sum1 + sum2;
    println!("{}", sum);
}
```

Designing Parallel Algorithms From Scratch

Designing a parallel algorithm from scratch involves several steps, including:

- Identify the problem and determine if it is suitable for parallelization. Some problems are naturally parallelizable, while others may be more difficult or impossible to parallelize. It is important to carefully consider the characteristics of the problem and the available hardware and software resources before deciding to implement a parallel algorithm.

- Break the problem into smaller, independent subproblems. In order to take advantage of parallelism, it is often necessary to decompose the problem into smaller, independent subproblems that can be solved concurrently.

- Choose a parallelism library or API. There are several options available in Rust, including rayon, rayon::join, and std::thread. Each has its own strengths and weaknesses, and the choice will depend on the specific needs of the algorithm.

- Implement the algorithm using the chosen parallelism library or API. This will typically involve dividing the input data into chunks, spawning threads or tasks to process the chunks concurrently, and combining the results at the end.

- Test and debug the algorithm. It is important to thoroughly test the algorithm to ensure that it is correct and performs well. Debugging parallel algorithms can be more challenging than debugging sequential algorithms, due to the added complexity of concurrent execution.

Here is a simple example of how you might design a parallel algorithm from scratch using the rayon crate:

```rust
use rayon::prelude::*;

fn sum_of_squares(n: u32) -> u32 {
    // Divide the input into chunks of size 10.
    (0..n).into_par_iter().chunks(10).map(|chunk| {
        // Calculate the sum of the squares of the numbers in
each chunk.
        chunk.map(|i| i * i).sum::<u32>()
    }).sum()
}

fn main() {
    let sum = sum_of_squares(100);
    println!("{}", sum);
}
```

This algorithm calculates the sum of the squares of the first n integers by dividing the input into chunks of size 10 and calculating the sum of the squares of the numbers in each chunk concurrently. The results are then combined at the end using the sum method.

Recipe#5: Debugging and Testing Concurrent Programs

Tips and Techniques to Test and Debug

Debugging and testing concurrent programs in Rust can be challenging due to the added complexity of concurrent execution. Following are some helpful tips and techniques that can help:

- Use Rust's built-in debugging tools: Rust provides a number of tools for debugging concurrent programs, including the debug_assert! and debug_assert_eq! macros, the dbg!

macro, and the #[cfg(debug_assertions)] attribute. These can be very useful for quickly identifying and fixing issues in concurrent code.

- Use the std::sync::atomic module: The std::sync::atomic module provides a number of types and functions for working with atomic variables, which can be used to implement low-level, lock-free synchronization. These can be helpful for debugging concurrent programs by providing a way to ensure that certain invariants are upheld.

- Use the rayon crate: The rayon crate provides a number of parallel iterators and other parallel algorithms that can be helpful for testing concurrent programs. For example, you can use the par_bridge iterator to wrap a sequential iterator and test its behavior in a concurrent context.

- Use the crossbeam crate: The crossbeam crate provides a number of useful tools for concurrent programming, including concurrent data structures, synchronization primitives, and parallel iterators. It also includes a scope module that can be used to spawn threads and tasks within a scope, making it easier to manage and debug concurrent code.

Debugging Using 'rayon' and 'crossbeam'

Following is a sample program on how you might use the rayon and crossbeam crates to test a concurrent algorithm:

```rust
use rayon::prelude::*;
use crossbeam::thread;

fn sum_of_squares(n: u32) -> u32 {
    (0..n).into_par_iter().map(|i| i * i).sum()
}

#[test]
fn test_sum_of_squares() {
    let n = 100;
    let expected = (0..n).map(|i| i * i).sum();
```

```
    // Test the algorithm in a single-threaded context.
    assert_eq!(sum_of_squares(n), expected);

    // Test the algorithm in a multi-threaded context.
    thread::scope(|s| {
        s.spawn(|_| {
            assert_eq!(sum_of_squares(n), expected);
        });
        s.spawn(|_| {
            assert_eq!(sum_of_squares(n), expected);
        });
    }).unwrap();
}
```

This code defines a sum_of_squares function that calculates the sum of the squares of the first n integers using a parallel iterator from the rayon crate. It then defines a test function that tests the behavior of the algorithm in both a single-threaded and multi-threaded context using the thread::scope function from the crossbeam crate.

Recipe#6: Optimizing Concurrent Programs

Procedure Steps to Rust Optimization

Optimizing concurrent programs in Rust involves several steps, including:

- Identify the performance bottlenecks: The first step in optimizing a concurrent program is to identify the performance bottlenecks, or areas of the code that are taking the most time to execute. This can be done using tools such as Rust's built-in profiler, or by manually analyzing the code and measuring the execution time of different sections.

- Choose the right synchronization mechanism: Choosing the right synchronization mechanism can have a big impact on the performance of a concurrent program. For example, using a mutex can be slower than using an atomic variable, but it provides stronger guarantees about the behavior of the program. It is important to carefully consider the trade-offs and choose the mechanism that is most appropriate for the specific needs of the program.

- Use parallel algorithms and data structures: There are a number of parallel algorithms and data structures available in Rust that can help improve the performance of concurrent programs. For example, the rayon crate provides a wide range of parallel iterators and other parallel algorithms that can be used to parallelize computations. The crossbeam crate provides concurrent data structures such as Queue and Deque that can be used to improve the performance of concurrent programs.

- Tune the parameters of the concurrent program: There are a number of parameters that can be adjusted to optimize the performance of a concurrent program, including the number of threads or tasks to use, the size of the data chunks to process concurrently, and the amount of work to be done by each thread or task. It is often helpful to experiment with different combinations of these parameters to find the optimal configuration.

- Use hardware-specific optimization techniques: Some hardware architectures are better suited to certain types of concurrent programs than others. For example, programs that rely heavily on atomic operations may perform better on architectures with strong support for atomic instructions, such as x86. It can be helpful to take advantage of hardware-specific optimization techniques to further improve the performance of concurrent programs.

Optimizing Rust Program Using Rayon

Here is a simple example of how you might optimize a concurrent program in Rust using the rayon crate:

```rust
use rayon::prelude::*;

fn sum_of_squares(n: u32) -> u32 {
    (0..n).into_par_iter().map(|i| i * i).sum()
}
```

```rust
fn main() {
    let n = 1_000_000;
    let sum = sum_of_squares(n);
    println!("{}", sum);
}
```

This program calculates the sum of the squares of the first n integers using a parallel iterator from the rayon crate. To optimize this program, we might try the following:

Identify the performance bottlenecks: We can use Rust's built-in profiler or manually analyze the code to identify the performance bottlenecks. In this case, the main bottleneck is likely to be the calculation of the sum of the squares.

Choose the right synchronization mechanism: Since we are not using any explicit synchronization mechanisms in this program, there is no need to choose a specific mechanism.

Use parallel algorithms and data structures: We are already using a parallel iterator from the rayon crate to parallelize the calculation of the sum of the squares. We could try using other parallel algorithms or data structures from rayon or other crates to see if they improve the performance of the program.

Tune the parameters of the concurrent program: We can try adjusting the number of threads used by the parallel iterator to see if it improves the performance of the program. We can also try adjusting the size of the data chunks processed concurrently by the iterator.

Use hardware-specific optimization techniques: If we are running the program on a specific hardware architecture, we can try using hardware-specific optimization techniques to improve the performance. For example, if the architecture has strong support for atomic instructions, we might try using atomic variables to implement the sum of the squares in a lock-free way.

Recipe#7: Dealing with Deadlocks and Livelocks

Understanding Deadlocks and Livelocks

Deadlocks and livelocks are two common problems that can occur when working with concurrent programs.

A deadlock occurs when two or more threads are blocked and waiting for each other, resulting in a situation where none of the threads can make progress. This can happen when each thread is holding a lock on a resource that the other thread needs, and is waiting for the other thread to release the lock. Following is a sample program of a simple program that can deadlock:

```rust
use std::sync::{Mutex, Arc};
use std::thread;

fn main() {
    let mutex1 = Arc::new(Mutex::new(0));
    let mutex2 = Arc::new(Mutex::new(0));

    let mutex1_clone = mutex1.clone();
    let mutex2_clone = mutex2.clone();

    let handle = thread::spawn(move || {
        let _lock1 = mutex1_clone.lock().unwrap();
        let _lock2 = mutex2_clone.lock().unwrap();
        // Do some work...
    });

    let _lock1 = mutex1.lock().unwrap();
    let _lock2 = mutex2.lock().unwrap();
    // Do some work...
```

```
        handle.join().unwrap();
}
```

In this example, the main thread acquires a lock on mutex1 and then tries to acquire a lock on mutex2. At the same time, the spawned thread acquires a lock on mutex2 and then tries to acquire a lock on mutex1. As a result, both threads are blocked and waiting for each other to release their locks, resulting in a deadlock.

A livelock is a situation where two or more threads are continuously trying to acquire locks or resources, but are unable to make progress because they keep yielding to each other. This can happen when each thread is trying to acquire a lock that is held by the other thread, and is repeatedly yielding to the other thread in the hope that it will release the lock. Following is a sample program of a simple program that can livelock:

```
use std::sync::{Mutex, Arc};
use std::thread;
use std::time::Duration;

fn main() {
    let mutex1 = Arc::new(Mutex::new(0));
    let mutex2 = Arc::new(Mutex::new(0));

    let mutex1_clone = mutex1.clone();
    let mutex2_clone = mutex2.clone();

    let handle = thread::spawn(move || {
        loop {
            let lock1 = mutex1_clone.lock();
            if lock1.is_ok() {
                let lock2 = mutex2_clone.lock();
                if lock2.is_ok() {
                    // Do some work...
                    break;
```

```rust
                } else {
                    thread::yield_now();
                }
            } else {
                thread::yield_now();
            }
        }
    });

    loop {
        let lock1 = mutex1.lock();
        if lock1.is_ok() {
            let lock2 = mutex2.lock();
            if lock2.is_ok() {
                // Do some work...
                break;
            } else {
                thread::yield_now();
            }
        } else {
            thread::yield_now();
        }
    }

    handle.join().unwrap();
}
```

In this example, both the main thread and the spawned thread are trying to acquire locks on mutex1 and mutex2 in a loop. If they are unable to acquire a lock, they yield to the other thread in the hope that it will release the lock. This can result in a situation where both threads are continuously yielding to each other, resulting in a livelock.

To deal with deadlocks and livelocks, it is important to carefully design the concurrent program to avoid these situations. This can involve using different synchronization mechanisms, such as mutexes, atomic variables, or lock-free data structures, or using techniques such as lock ordering to avoid deadlocks. It can also involve adding timeouts to lock acquisitions to avoid livelocks, or using techniques such as backoff to reduce contention for resources.

CHAPTER 6: ASYNCHRONOUS PROGRAMMING

Recipe#1: Defining Asynchronous Functions

Async Keyword

In Rust, you can define asynchronous functions using the async keyword. Asynchronous functions return a value of type Future, which represents a value that may not be available yet. You can use the await keyword to block on the completion of an asynchronous operation within the function.

Programming Asynchronous Function

Following is a sample program on an asynchronous function that returns a Future:

```rust
use futures::future::Future;

async fn foo() -> u32 {
    // Perform some asynchronous work.
    let value = do_something().await;

    // Return a value.
    value + 1
}
```

To use the foo function, you can call it and use the .await operator to block on the returned Future:

```rust
use futures::executor::block_on;

fn main() {
    let result = block_on(foo());
    println!("Result: {}", result);
}
```

You can also use the .then method on the Future to set up a callback to be executed when the Future completes:

```rust
use futures::future::Future;

async fn foo() -> u32 {
    // Perform some asynchronous work.
    let value = do_something().await;

    // Return a value.
    value + 1
}

fn main() {
    let future = foo().then(|result| {
        println!("Result: {}", result);
        Ok(())
    });

    // Run the future to completion.

tokio::runtime::Runtime::new().unwrap().block_on(future);
}
```

You can use asynchronous functions in combination with executors, such as tokio or async-std, to run multiple asynchronous tasks concurrently.

Recipe#2: Run Asynchronous Tasks

Executor

To run asynchronous tasks in Rust, you can use an executor, which is a runtime component that schedules asynchronous tasks to be run. There are several executors available for Rust, including tokio, async-std, and smol.

Using Tokio for Asynchronous Tasks

Following is a sample program on how you can use the tokio executor to run an asynchronous task:

```rust
use tokio::task;

async fn foo() {
    // Perform some asynchronous work.
    do_something().await;
}

fn main() {
    // Spawn the `foo` task.
    task::spawn(foo());

    // Run the executor.
    tokio::runtime::Runtime::new().unwrap().run().unwrap();
}
```

This example creates an asynchronous task using the foo function and spawns it using the task::spawn function. It then creates a tokio runtime and runs it using the run method. This will run the foo task to completion.

You can also use the .await operator to block on the completion of an asynchronous task:

```rust
use tokio::task;

async fn foo() -> u32 {
    // Perform some asynchronous work.
    do_something().await;

    // Return a value.
    42
}

fn main() {
    // Spawn the `foo` task.
    let future = task::spawn(foo());

    // Block on the task and print the result.
    let                             result                              =
tokio::runtime::Runtime::new().unwrap().block_on(future);
    println!("Result: {}", result);
}
```

This example creates an asynchronous task using the foo function and spawns it using the task::spawn function. It then blocks on the task using the block_on method and prints the result.

Recipe#3: Error Handling

Result Type: Ok and Err

In Rust, you can use the Result type to handle errors that may occur during the execution of your program. The Result type is an enumeration with two variants: Ok, which represents a successful result, and Err, which represents a failure.

Handling Errors Using Result Type

Following is a sample program on how you can use the Result type to handle errors:

```rust
use std::fs;
use std::io;

fn read_file(filename: &str) -> Result<String, io::Error> {
    // Open the file.
    let mut file = match fs::File::open(filename) {
        Ok(file) => file,
        Err(e) => return Err(e),
    };

    // Read the contents of the file.
    let mut contents = String::new();
    match file.read_to_string(&mut contents) {
        Ok(_) => Ok(contents),
        Err(e) => Err(e),
    }
}

fn main() {
    // Call the function and handle the result.
    match read_file("file.txt") {
        Ok(contents)   =>   println!("File   contents:   {}", contents),
        Err(e) => println!("Error: {}", e),
    }
}
```

In this example, the read_file function returns a Result with a String as the Ok variant and an io::Error as the Err variant. The function tries to open the file and reads its contents, returning the contents as a String on success

You can use the ? operator to simplify the error handling process. The ? operator allows you to propagate errors through a chain of function calls and automatically return an Err value if an error occurs.

Following is a sample program on how you can use the ? operator to handle errors:

```rust
use std::fs;
use std::io;

fn read_file(filename: &str) -> Result<String, io::Error> {
    // Open the file.
    let mut file = fs::File::open(filename)?;

    // Read the contents of the file.
    let mut contents = String::new();
    file.read_to_string(&mut contents)?;

    Ok(contents)
}

fn main() {
    // Call the function and handle the result.
    match read_file("file.txt") {
        Ok(contents) => println!("File contents: {}", contents),
        Err(e) => println!("Error: {}", e),
    }
}
```

In this example, the read_file function uses the ? operator to propagate any errors that occur when opening the file or reading its contents. If an error occurs, the ? operator will automatically return an Err value, otherwise it will return the Ok value.

You can also use the From trait to convert an error type into another type. This can be useful if you want to return a custom error type from your function instead of a type from the standard library.

For example:

```rust
use std::fs;
use std::io;

#[derive(Debug)]
enum CustomError {
    IoError(io::Error),
    ParseError(std::num::ParseIntError),
}

impl From<io::Error> for CustomError {
    fn from(error: io::Error) -> Self {
        CustomError::IoError(error)
    }
}

impl From<std::num::ParseIntError> for CustomError {
    fn from(error: std::num::ParseIntError) -> Self {
        CustomError::ParseError(error)
    }
}

fn read_file(filename: &str) -> Result<i32, CustomError> {
    // Open the file.
    let                     contents                     =
fs::read_to_string(filename).map_err(CustomError::from)?;
```

```rust
    // Parse the contents of the file.
    let                    value:                   i32                =
contents.trim().parse().map_err(CustomError::from)?;

    Ok(value)
}


fn main() {
    // Call the function and handle the result.
    match read_file("file.txt") {
        Ok(value) => println!("Value: {}", value),
        Err(e) => println!("Error: {:?}", e),
    }
}
```

In this example, the read_file function uses the map_err method to convert any io::Error or std::num::ParseIntError values into a CustomError value. The map_err method is called on the Result value returned by fs::read_to_string and contents.trim().parse, and it applies the provided closure to the

Recipe#4: Debugging Asynchronous Code

Tokio-test Crate

Debugging asynchronous code can be challenging, as it can be difficult to understand the order in which tasks are being executed and how they are interacting with each other. However, there are a number of tools and techniques available to help with debugging asynchronous code in Rust.

One tool that can be helpful for debugging asynchronous code is the tokio-test crate, which provides utilities for testing asynchronous code. The tokio-test crate allows you to test asynchronous functions by running them to completion and asserting on the result.

Testing Asynchronous Functions

Following is a sample program on how you can use the tokio-test crate to test an asynchronous function:

```rust
use tokio::task;
use tokio_test::assert_pending;
use tokio_test::block_on;

#[tokio::test]
async fn test_foo() {
    // Define the asynchronous function to test.
    async fn foo() -> u32 {
        // Perform some asynchronous work.
        let value = do_something().await;

        // Return a value.
        value + 1
    }

    // Spawn the `foo` task.
    let future = task::spawn(foo());

    // Assert that the task is pending.
    assert_pending!(future);

    // Run the task to completion.
    let result = block_on(future);

    // Assert on the result.
```

```
    assert_eq!(result, 42);
}
```

In this example, the test_foo function tests the foo asynchronous function by spawning it as a task and using the assert_pending! macro to assert that the task is pending. It then runs the task to completion using the block_on function and asserts on the result using the assert_eq! macro.

Another option for debugging asynchronous code is to use the futures::executor::ThreadPool executor, which allows you to run asynchronous tasks on a dedicated thread pool. This can be helpful for debugging because it allows you to inspect the state of the tasks and the thread pool using a debugger.

Following is a sample program on how you can use the ThreadPool executor to debug asynchronous code:

```rust
use futures::executor::ThreadPool;
use futures::future::Future;

fn main() {
    // Create a thread pool with a single thread.
    let mut pool = ThreadPool::new().unwrap();

    // Define the asynchronous function to debug.
    async fn foo() -> u32 {
        // Perform some asynchronous work.
        let value = do_something().await;

        // Return a value.
        value + 1
    }

    // Spawn the `foo` task on the thread pool.
    let future = pool.spawn_with_handle(foo());
```

```
    // Run the task to completion.
    let result = pool.run(future);

    // Inspect the result using a debugger.
    let _ = result;
}
```

In this example, the foo asynchronous function is spawned on a thread pool using the spawn_with_handle method. The ThreadPool executor allows you to run the task to completion using the run method, and you can then use a debugger to inspect the result.

Recipe#5: Working with Asynchronous I/O

I/O Operations

Asynchronous I/O is a common use case for asynchronous programming, as it allows you to perform I/O operations without blocking the current thread. Rust provides a number of libraries for working with asynchronous I/O, such as tokio, async-std, and futures-io.

Performing Asynchronous I/O using Tokio

Following is a sample program on how you can use the tokio library to perform asynchronous I/O in Rust:

```
use tokio::fs;

#[tokio::main]
async fn main() -> Result<(), Box<dyn std::error::Error>> {
```

```rust
    // Read the contents of a file.
    let contents = fs::read_to_string("file.txt").await?;
    println!("File contents: {}", contents);

    // Write to a file.
    fs::write("output.txt", "Hello, world!").await?;

    Ok(())
}
```

In this example, the read_to_string function is used to asynchronously read the contents of a file, and the write function is used to asynchronously write to a file. The .await operator is used to block on the completion of the asynchronous operations. You can also use the async-std library to perform asynchronous I/O in Rust.

Following is a sample program on how you can use the async-std library to perform asynchronous I/O with a file:

```rust
use async_std::fs;

#[async_std::main]
async fn main() -> Result<(), Box<dyn std::error::Error>> {
    // Read the contents of a file.
    let contents = fs::read_to_string("file.txt").await?;
    println!("File contents: {}", contents);

    // Write to a file.
    fs::write("output.txt", "Hello, world!").await?;

    Ok(())
}
```

In this example, the read_to_string function is used to asynchronously read the contents of a file, and the write function is used to asynchronously write to a file. The .await operator is used to block on the completion of the asynchronous operations.

Recipe#6: Working with Channels and MPSC/SPSC Communication Patterns

Channels: MPSC and SPSC

Channels are a way of communicating between asynchronous tasks in Rust. They allow you to send values from one task to another, and they can be used to coordinate the execution of asynchronous tasks. There are two main types of channels in Rust: multiple producer, single consumer (MPSC) channels and single producer, single consumer (SPSC) channels.

Using Channel Function to Create MPSC (Multiple Producer, Single Consumer)

Following is a sample program on how you can use the futures crate's channel function to create an MPSC channel in Rust:

```rust
use futures::channel::mpsc;
use futures::{future, FutureExt};

#[tokio::main]
async fn main() {
    // Create an MPSC channel.
    let (mut sender, mut receiver) = mpsc::channel(10);

    // Spawn a task to send values to the channel.
```

```
tokio::spawn(async move {
    for i in 0..10 {
        sender.send(i).await.unwrap();
    }
});

// Receive values from the channel in the main task.
while let Some(val) = receiver.next().await {
    println!("Received value: {}", val);
}
}
```

In this example, the mpsc::channel function is used to create an MPSC channel with a capacity of 10. A task is spawned to send values to the channel using the send method, and the main task receives values from the channel using the next method.

Following is a sample program on how you can use the futures crate's unbounded_channel function to create an SPSC channel in Rust:

```
use futures::channel::mpsc;
use futures::{future, FutureExt};

#[tokio::main]
async fn main() {
    // Create an SPSC channel.
    let (mut sender, mut receiver) = mpsc::unbounded_channel();

    // Spawn a task to send values to the channel.
    tokio::spawn(async move {
        for i in 0..10 {
            sender.send(i).await.unwrap();
        }
```

```
    });

    // Receive values from the channel in the main task.
    while let Some(val) = receiver.next().await {
        println!("Received value: {}", val);
    }
}
```

In this example, the mpsc::unbounded_channel function is used to create an SPSC channel with an unlimited capacity. A task is spawned to send values to the channel using the send method, and the main task receives values from the channel using the next method.

Recipe#7: Implementing Asynchronous Networking

Tasks of Asynchronous Networking

Asynchronous networking is a common use case for asynchronous programming, as it allows you to perform network operations without blocking the current thread. Rust provides a number of libraries for implementing asynchronous networking, such as tokio, async-std, and futures-io.

Implementing Asynchronous Networking

Following is a sample program on how you can use the tokio library to implement asynchronous networking in Rust:

```
use tokio::net::TcpListener;
use tokio::prelude::*;
```

```rust
#[tokio::main]
async fn main() -> Result<(), Box<dyn std::error::Error>> {
    // Bind a TCP listener to a local address.
    let mut listener =
TcpListener::bind("127.0.0.1:8080").await?;

    // Accept incoming connections in a loop.
    loop {
        // Asynchronously wait for a new connection.
        let (mut socket, _) = listener.accept().await?;

        // Spawn a task to handle the connection.
        tokio::spawn(async move {
            // Read data from the socket.
            let mut buf = [0; 1024];
            let n = socket.read(&mut buf).await.unwrap();
            println!("Read {} bytes from the socket.", n);

            // Write data to the socket.
            socket.write_all(b"Hello,
world!").await.unwrap();
        });
    }
}
```

In this example, the TcpListener::bind function is used to bind a TCP listener to a local address, and the accept method is used to asynchronously wait for new connections. When a new connection is accepted, a task is spawned to handle the connection using the tokio::spawn function. The task reads data from the socket using the read method and writes data to the socket using the write_all method.

You can also use the async-std library to implement asynchronous networking in Rust. Following is a sample program on how you can use the async-std library to implement a simple TCP echo server:

```rust
use async_std::net::{TcpListener, TcpStream};
use async_std::prelude::*;

#[async_std::main]
async fn main() -> Result<(), Box<dyn std::error::Error>> {
    // Bind a TCP listener to a local address.
    let                  mut                  listener                  =
TcpListener::bind("127.0.0.1:8080").await?;

    // Accept incoming connections in a loop.
    while let Ok((mut socket, _)) = listener.accept().await
{
        // Spawn a task to handle the connection.
        async_std::task::spawn(async move {
            // Read data from the socket.
            let mut buf = [0; 1024];
            let n = socket.read(&mut buf).await.unwrap();
            println!("Read {} bytes from the socket.", n);

            // Write the data back to the socket.
            socket.write_all(&buf[..n]).await.unwrap();
        });
    }

    Ok(())
}
```

In this example, the TcpListener::bind function is used to bind a TCP listener to a local address, and the accept method is used to asynchronously wait for new connections. When a new connection is accepted, a task is spawned to handle the connection using the async_std::task::spawn function. The task reads data from the socket using the read method and writes the data back to the socket using the write_all method.

Recipe#8: Integrate with Asynchronous Libraries

Tools and Techniques for Integration

Integrating with asynchronous libraries in Rust can be challenging, as it requires coordinating the asynchronous tasks of the different libraries. However, there are a number of tools and techniques available to help with this process.

One tool that can be helpful for integrating with asynchronous libraries is the tokio-sync crate, which provides synchronization primitives such as Mutex, RwLock, and Barrier that can be used to coordinate asynchronous tasks.

Using tokio-sync to Integrate Asynchronous Tasks

Following is a sample program on how you can use the tokio-sync crate to coordinate asynchronous tasks:

```rust
use tokio::sync::{Mutex, RwLock};
use tokio::task;

#[tokio::main]
async fn main() {
    // Create a mutex to protect shared data.
    let mutex = Mutex::new(0);

    // Spawn two tasks that increment the shared data.
    let mut handles = Vec::new();
    for _ in 0..2 {
        let mutex = mutex.clone();
        let handle = task::spawn(async move {
            let mut data = mutex.lock().await;
            *data += 1;
```

```
    });
    handles.push(handle);
}

// Wait for the tasks to complete.
for handle in handles {
    handle.await.unwrap();
}

// Read the final value of the shared data.
let data = mutex.lock().await;
println!("Final value: {}", *data);
}
```

In this example, the Mutex is used to protect a shared piece of data and coordinate access to it between two asynchronous tasks. The tasks acquire the mutex using the lock method and increment the shared data, and the main task waits for the tasks to complete using the await operator.

Another option for integrating with asynchronous libraries is to use the futures crate, which provides a number of combinators for working with asynchronous tasks.

Following is a sample program on how you can use the futures crate to coordinate asynchronous tasks:

```
use futures::{future, FutureExt};

#[tokio::main]
async fn main() {
    // Define two asynchronous tasks.
    let task1 = async { 1 };
    let task2 = async { 2 };

    // Run the tasks in parallel and wait for them to
complete.
```

```rust
    let result = future::join(task1, task2).await;

    // Print the results of the tasks.
    println!("Result: {:?}", result);
}
```

In this example, the join combinator is used to run the task1 and task2 tasks in parallel and wait for them to complete. The await operator is used to block on the completion of the join future, and the results of the tasks are printed using the println! macro.

CHAPTER 7: DEVELOPING REST AND SOAP APIs

Recipe#1: Creating SOAP APIs

What are SOAP API?

SOAP (Simple Object Access Protocol) is a protocol for exchanging structured information in the implementation of web services in computer networks. It uses XML (Extensible Markup Language) to encode messages, and it is designed to be extensible, neutral (able to operate over the Internet), and independent (not tied to any particular operating system or programming language).

SOAP APIs are APIs that use the SOAP protocol to communicate between systems. They are typically used to enable communication between different systems or applications over the web or other networks. SOAP APIs are often used to expose the functionality of a system or application to other systems or applications, allowing them to interact with each other and exchange data.

SOAP APIs are typically used when there is a need for a more formal and standardized approach to communication between systems, as SOAP defines a strict set of rules and conventions for encoding and transmitting messages. SOAP APIs are also often used when security is a concern, as SOAP supports various security mechanisms such as SSL and WS-Security.

Overall, SOAP APIs are a common approach for enabling communication and interoperability between systems and applications over the web or other networks.

Benefits of SOAP API -

There are several benefits to using SOAP APIs:
- Extensibility: SOAP is designed to be extensible, meaning that it can be extended with additional features and functionality as needed. This allows SOAP APIs to be customized and adapted to meet the specific needs of a system or application.
- Neutrality: SOAP is designed to be neutral, meaning that it can operate over the Internet and is not tied to any particular operating system or programming language. This makes SOAP

APIs suitable for use in a wide range of environments and scenarios.

- Independence: SOAP is designed to be independent, meaning that it is not tied to any particular operating system or programming language. This allows SOAP APIs to be used in a variety of different systems and applications, regardless of their underlying technology.
- Security: SOAP supports various security mechanisms, such as SSL and WS-Security, which can be used to secure SOAP APIs and protect sensitive data.
- Formalization: SOAP defines a strict set of rules and conventions for encoding and transmitting messages, which can help to ensure that SOAP APIs are used consistently and predictably.

Overall, the benefits of SOAP APIs include extensibility, neutrality, independence, security, and formalization, making them a useful choice for many types of systems and applications.

Creating SOP API Using 'xml-Rs'

Following is a sample program on how you might use Rust to create a SOAP API:

First, you would define the structure of the request and response messages for your API using the xml-rs crate:

```rust
use xml::{reader::XmlReader, writer::XmlWriter};
use xml::Event;

#[derive(Debug, Default)]
struct Request {
    // define request fields here
}

#[derive(Debug, Default)]
struct Response {
    // define response fields here
}
```

```rust
impl Request {
    fn from_xml(reader: &mut XmlReader<'_>) -> Result<Self,
String> {
        // parse request from XML reader and return result
    }
}


impl Response {
    fn to_xml<W: XmlWriter>(&self, writer: &mut W) ->
Result<(), String> {
        // write response to XML writer and return result
    }
}
```

Next, you would define a function that handles the request and returns a response:

```rust
use soap::{Error, Fault, SoapVersion, Transport};
use xml::{reader::XmlReader, writer::XmlWriter};

fn handle_request<'a>(
    reader: &mut XmlReader<'_>,
    writer: &mut XmlWriter<'a>,
) -> Result<(), Error> {
    let                          request                          =
Request::from_xml(reader).map_err(Fault::from)?;
    let response = Response::default(); // generate response
    response.to_xml(writer).map_err(Fault::from)?;
    Ok(())
}
```

Finally, you would use the soap crate to create a SOAP server that listens for incoming requests and uses the handle_request function to handle them:

```rust
use soap::{
    error::{Error, Result},
    http_transport::{HttpServer, HttpTransport},
    server::{Server, ServerBuilder},
};
use std::net::SocketAddr;

fn main() -> Result<()> {
    let server = HttpServer::new(SocketAddr::from(([127, 0,
0, 1], 8080)));
    let transport = HttpTransport::new(server);
    let mut server = ServerBuilder::new(transport)
        .start_http(([127, 0, 0, 1], 8080))?;

    println!("SOAP server listening on {}", server.url());
    server.run()
}
```

This code creates an HTTP server that listens for incoming requests on the specified address and port, and it uses the HttpTransport type from the soap crate to handle the HTTP communication. The ServerBuilder type is then used to create a Server instance that can handle SOAP requests and responses, and the server is started using the start_http method.

Finally, the run method is called to start the server and listen for incoming requests. When a request is received, the server will use the handle_request function defined earlier to handle the request and generate a response.

Recipe#2: Building RESTful APIs

What are REST API?

REST (Representational State Transfer) is a software architectural style for building web services. It is designed to be simple, scalable, and flexible, and it is based on the idea of representing the state of a system or application using a set of resources that can be accessed and manipulated using a fixed set of operations (e.g., GET, POST, PUT, DELETE).

REST APIs are APIs that use the REST architectural style to expose the functionality of a system or application to other systems or applications. They are typically used to enable communication between different systems or applications over the web or other networks, and they are designed to be easy to use and flexible.

REST APIs are typically implemented using HTTP (Hypertext Transfer Protocol) and use HTTP methods (e.g., GET, POST, PUT, DELETE) to specify the operation to be performed on the resource. They are often designed to be self-describing, meaning that they include documentation and metadata about the resources and operations they expose, making it easy for developers to understand and use the API.

Overall, REST APIs are a popular choice for building web services and enabling communication between systems and applications over the web or other networks.

Benefits of REST API

There are several benefits to using REST APIs:

- Simplicity: REST is designed to be simple and easy to use, and REST APIs are typically easy to understand and use as well. This makes REST APIs a good choice for many types of systems and applications.
- Scalability: REST is designed to be scalable, meaning that it can support a large number of clients and handle a high volume of requests. This makes REST APIs suitable for use in

high-traffic systems and applications.

- Flexibility: REST is designed to be flexible and adaptable, and REST APIs can be customized and extended to meet the specific needs of a system or application.

- Interoperability: REST APIs are typically implemented using HTTP and can be accessed using any HTTP client, making them easy to use and compatible with a wide range of systems and applications.

- Self-describing: REST APIs are often designed to be self-describing, meaning that they include documentation and metadata about the resources and operations they expose. This makes it easier for developers to understand and use the API.

Overall, the benefits of REST APIs include simplicity, scalability, flexibility, interoperability, and self-describing nature, making them a useful choice for many types of systems and applications.

Building REST API Using 'serde'

Following is a sample program on how you might use Rust to build a REST API:

First, you would define the structure of the request and response data for your API using the serde crate:

```rust
use serde::{Deserialize, Serialize};

#[derive(Debug, Deserialize, Serialize)]
struct Request {
    // define request fields here
}

#[derive(Debug, Deserialize, Serialize)]
struct Response {
    // define response fields here
}
```

Next, you would define a function that handles the request and returns a response:

```rust
use actix_web::{web, HttpResponse};

async fn handle_request(request: web::Json<Request>) -> HttpResponse {
    let request = request.into_inner();
    let response = Response::default(); // generate response
    HttpResponse::Ok().json(response)
}
```

Finally, you would use the actix-web crate to create a web server that listens for incoming requests and uses the handle_request function to handle them:

```rust
use actix_web::{App, HttpServer};

#[actix_rt::main]
async fn main() -> std::io::Result<()> {
    HttpServer::new(|| {
        App::new().route("/api/endpoint",
web::post().to(handle_request))
    })
    .bind("127.0.0.1:8080")?
    .run()
    .await
}
```

This code creates an HTTP server that listens for incoming requests on the specified address and port, and it uses the App type from the actix-web crate to define a route for handling requests to the /api/endpoint URL. When a request is received, the server will use the handle_request function to handle the request and generate a response.

Recipe#3: Automating API Documentation

Rust Tools and Libraries for API Documentation

There are several tools and libraries in Rust that you can use to generate documentation for your APIs:

- rustdoc: rustdoc is the documentation generator for the Rust programming language. It can be used to generate documentation for Rust crates, including documentation for their APIs. rustdoc generates documentation in HTML format and includes features such as syntax highlighting, cross-referencing, and search functionality.

- cargo-docgen: cargo-docgen is a Rust crate that can be used to generate API documentation for Rust crates. It uses the rustdoc tool to generate the documentation, and it provides additional features such as customizable templates and the ability to generate documentation for multiple crates at once.

- sphinx-rust: sphinx-rust is a Rust crate that can be used to generate API documentation for Rust crates using the Sphinx documentation generator. It provides support for generating documentation in various formats, including HTML, LaTeX, and PDF, and it includes features such as syntax highlighting and cross-referencing.

These are just a few examples of tools and libraries that you can use to generate API documentation for Rust programs.

Automating API Documentation Using 'rustdoc'

Following is a sample program on how you might use the rustdoc tool to generate API documentation for a Rust crate:

First, you would add documentation comments to your code:

```
/// This is a struct that represents a request.
///
```

```rust
/// # Fields
///
/// * `field1`: The first field of the request.
/// * `field2`: The second field of the request.
#[derive(Debug)]
struct Request {
    field1: String,
    field2: i32,
}


/// This is a function that handles a request.
///
/// # Arguments
///
/// * `request`: The request to handle.
///
/// # Returns
///
/// A response to the request.
fn handle_request(request: Request) -> Response {
    // handle request and return response
}
```

Next, you would use the cargo doc command to generate the documentation for your crate:

```
cargo doc
```

This will generate the documentation for your crate in HTML format and save it in the target/doc directory. You can then open the documentation in a web browser to view it.

The rustdoc tool includes many features and options for generating and formatting documentation, including support for syntax highlighting, cross-referencing, and search functionality. You can use these features to customize and enhance the documentation for your crate.

Recipe#4: Managing API Orchestration

Need of API Orchestration

API orchestration refers to the process of coordinating multiple APIs to work together to achieve a specific goal. This might involve calling multiple APIs in a specific order, aggregating the results of multiple APIs, or routing requests to the appropriate API based on certain conditions.

API orchestration is often needed in microservices architectures, where a single application is built as a collection of smaller, independent services. Each service may have its own API, and the APIs need to be orchestrated in order to provide a seamless experience to the end user.

API orchestration can also be useful in situations where you want to expose a single API to external clients, but the data or functionality needed to fulfill requests is spread across multiple backend systems. In this case, the API can act as a "front door" to the various backend systems, coordinating the necessary calls and aggregating the results as needed.

Overall, API orchestration can help to simplify the integration of multiple APIs and improve the efficiency of the system as a whole.

Managing API Orchestration Using Ocelot

Ocelot is a standalone API gateway written in Rust that can be used to manage API orchestration. Following is a sample program on how you might use Ocelot to orchestrate a simple API using the Actix web framework:

First, you'll need to add the necessary dependencies to your Cargo.toml file:

```
[dependencies]
actix-web = "2.0"
ocelot = "0.9"
```

Next, you'll need to define the API endpoint that you want to orchestrate. This example uses Actix to define a simple endpoint that returns a list of users:

```rust
use actix_web::{web, App, HttpServer, Responder};

#[actix_rt::main]
async fn main() -> std::io::Result<()> {
    HttpServer::new(|| {
        App::new()
            .route("/users", web::get().to(get_users))
    })
    .bind("127.0.0.1:8080")?
    .run()
    .await
}

async fn get_users() -> impl Responder {
    let users = vec![
        User {
            id: 1,
            name: "Alice".to_string(),
        },
        User {
            id: 2,
            name: "Bob".to_string(),
        },
        User {
            id: 3,
            name: "Charlie".to_string(),
        },
    ];
    web::Json(users)
}
```

Then, you'll need to configure Ocelot to manage the API orchestration. This can be done using a YAML configuration file, like this:

```yaml
global_config:
  base_url: "http://localhost:8080"

re_routes:
- downstream_path_template: "/users"
  downstream_scheme: "http"
  downstream_host_and_ports:
  - host: "localhost"
    port: 8080
  upstream_path_template: "/api/users"
  upstream_http_method: "GET"
```

This configuration tells Ocelot to route incoming requests to the /api/users endpoint to the /users endpoint on the downstream service (in this case, the Actix API we defined earlier).

Finally, you can start Ocelot using the following code:

```rust
use ocelot::{App, Config};

#[actix_rt::main]
async fn main() -> std::io::Result<()> {
    let config = Config::from_file("ocelot.yaml").unwrap();
    let app = App::new(config);
    app.start().await
}
```

With these steps, Ocelot will manage the orchestration of the API, routing requests from the /api/users endpoint to the downstream service and returning the results to the client.

Recipe#5: Adding Security to API

Need of Security to APIs

APIs need security to protect against a range of potential threats, including unauthorized access, data leakage, and denial of service attacks.

Here are a few specific reasons why API security is important:

- Confidentiality: APIs often expose sensitive data or functionality, such as personal information or financial transactions. Without proper security measures, this data could be accessed by unauthorized parties.
- Integrity: API security is necessary to ensure that data transmitted through the API has not been tampered with or modified in any way.
- Availability: APIs are critical to the operation of many modern systems, and a breach of API security could lead to a denial of service attack, disrupting the availability of the API and the systems that depend on it.
- Compliance: Many industries have strict regulations around the handling of sensitive data, and API security is necessary to ensure compliance with these regulations.

Overall, API security is important to protect against a variety of threats and to ensure that APIs are used in a safe and secure manner.

Ways to Secure APIs

There are several ways you can add security to an API built with Rust. Here are a few options:

- Use a web framework with built-in security features: Many Rust web frameworks, such as Actix and Rocket, provide built-in support for common security features such as SSL/TLS, authentication, and authorization.
- Use a standalone security library: There are several libraries available for Rust that provide specific security-related functionality, such as Argon2 for password hashing and ring for

cryptography.

- Use a reverse proxy: A reverse proxy sits between your API and the internet, handling tasks such as SSL termination, authentication, and authorization. There are several reverse proxy options available for Rust, including Envoy and Traefik.

- Use a combination of the above approaches: Depending on your specific needs, you may find that it makes sense to use a combination of these approaches. For example, you could use a web framework to handle SSL and basic authentication, and then use a reverse proxy for more advanced security features such as rate limiting and request filtering.

Ultimately, the best approach for adding security to your API will depend on your specific requirements and the resources available to you.

Securing API Using Actix

Following is a sample program on how you might use the Actix web framework to add basic authentication to your Rust API:

First, you'll need to add the necessary dependencies to your Cargo.toml file:

```
[dependencies]
actix-web = "2.0"
actix-web-auth = "0.3"
```

Next, you'll need to define the API endpoint that you want to secure. This example uses Actix to define a simple endpoint that returns a list of users:

```
use actix_web::{web, App, HttpServer, Responder};

#[actix_rt::main]
async fn main() -> std::io::Result<()> {
    HttpServer::new(|| {
        App::new()
```

```rust
            .route("/users", web::get().to(get_users))
    })
    .bind("127.0.0.1:8080")?
    .run()
    .await
}

async fn get_users() -> impl Responder {
    let users = vec![
        User {
            id: 1,
            name: "Alice".to_string(),
        },
        User {
            id: 2,
            name: "Bob".to_string(),
        },
        User {
            id: 3,
            name: "Charlie".to_string(),
        },
    ];
    web::Json(users)
}
```

Then, you can use the actix-web-auth library to add basic authentication to the API endpoint. Following is a sample program on how you might do this:

```rust
use actix_web::{web, App, HttpServer, Responder};
use actix_web_auth::basic::{BasicAuth, BasicAuthMiddleware};

#[actix_rt::main]
async fn main() -> std::io::Result<()> {
    let    auth   =    BasicAuth::new("my-realm",    |username,
```

```rust
password| {
        if username == "user" && password == "pass" {
            Ok(username.to_string())
        } else {
            Err(())
        }
    });

    HttpServer::new(|| {
        App::new()
            .wrap(BasicAuthMiddleware::new(auth))
            .route("/users", web::get().to(get_users))
    })
    .bind("127.0.0.1:8080")?
    .run()
    .await
}

async fn get_users() -> impl Responder {
    let users = vec![
        User {
            id: 1,
            name: "Alice".to_string(),
        },
        User {
            id: 2,
            name: "Bob".to_string(),
        },
        User {
            id: 3,
            name: "Charlie".to_string(),
        },
    ];
    web::Json(users)
```

```
}
```

With these changes, the API will require basic authentication for the /users endpoint. When a client makes a request to this endpoint, the server will expect an Authorization header with a valid username and password, and will return a 401 Unauthorized response if the header is not present or the credentials are invalid.

Following is a sample program on how a client might make a request to the secured API endpoint:

```rust
use actix_web::{client, web, App, HttpResponse, HttpServer};
use base64;
use std::env;

#[actix_rt::main]
async fn main() -> std::io::Result<()> {
    let username = env::var("USERNAME").unwrap();
    let password = env::var("PASSWORD").unwrap();
    let auth = base64::encode(&format!("{}:{}", username,
password));

    let client = client::Client::new();
    let response = client
        .get("http://localhost:8080/users")
        .header("Authorization", format!("Basic {}", auth))
        .send()
        .await
        .unwrap();

    println!("Response: {}", response.status());
    println!("Body: {}", response.body().await.unwrap());
}
```

This code uses the actix-web client library to make a request to the /users endpoint, passing the necessary Authorization header with a base64-encoded version of the username and password. The server will then validate the credentials and either allow or deny access to the endpoint based on the result.

Recipe#6: Monitoring API

API Performance Monitoring

There are several ways to do performance monitoring of an API written in Rust. One option is to use a dedicated performance monitoring tool, such as Prometheus, which can collect metrics from your API and provide visualization and alerting capabilities.

To use Prometheus with a Rust API, you can use the prometheus crate, which provides an API for exposing metrics in the Prometheus format. Following is a sample program on how you can use it:

```rust
use prometheus::{self, Encoder, Registry, TextEncoder};

// Create a registry to hold the metrics.
let registry = Registry::new();

// Create a new counter metric and increment it when handling
a request.
let counter = prometheus::Counter::new("requests_total",
"Total number of requests served.").unwrap();
registry.register(Box::new(counter)).unwrap();

// Increment the counter when handling a request.
counter.inc();

// Expose the metrics over HTTP.
```

```rust
let encoder = TextEncoder::new();
let metric_families = registry.gather();
let mut buffer = vec![];
encoder.encode(&metric_families, &mut buffer).unwrap();

// Serve the metrics at `/metrics` endpoint.
rocket::ignite()
    .mount("/metrics", routes![metrics])
    .launch();

#[get("/metrics")]
fn metrics() -> rocket::response::content::Html<String> {
    let mut output = String::new();
    for s in buffer.iter() {
        output.push_str(str::from_utf8(s).unwrap());
    }
    rocket::response::content::Html(output)
}
```

This will expose the metrics at the /metrics endpoint, which can be scraped by Prometheus. You can then use Prometheus to visualize and alert on the collected metrics.

Monitoring Errors In API

There are several ways to monitor errors in a Rust API. One option is to use a dedicated error monitoring tool, such as Sentry, which can collect error logs from your API and provide visualization and alerting capabilities.

To use Sentry with a Rust API, you can use the sentry crate, which provides an API for sending error logs to Sentry. Following is a sample program on how you can use it:

```rust
use sentry::integrations::failure::capture_error;
use sentry::{Event, Level};
```

```rust
fn main() {
    // Initialize the Sentry client.

sentry::init("https://YOUR_SENTRY_DSN@sentry.io/YOUR_PROJEC
T_ID");

    // Capture an error and send it to Sentry.
    let event_id = capture_error(|_| {
        // Your code here.
        Event::new().level(Level::Error).message("Something
went wrong!")
    });

    // You can use the event ID to check the status of the
event on Sentry.
    println!("Event ID: {}", event_id);
}
```

This will send any errors that are captured by the capture_error closure to Sentry, where you can view and alert on them.

Another option is to use Rust's built-in error handling mechanisms, such as the Result type and the ? operator, to handle and log errors in your API. For example:

```rust
fn handle_request() -> Result<Response, Error> {
    // Your code here.
    let result = do_something().map_err(|e| {
        error!("Error occurred: {}", e);
        e
    })?;
    Ok(Response::new(result))
}
```

This will log any errors that occur in the do_something function and return a Result that can be used to handle the error appropriately. You can also use a logging library, such as log or env_logger, to output the logs to a file or other destination for further analysis.

Checking API Usage

There are several ways to monitor and control API usage in Rust. One option is to use a rate limiting library, such as throttle, which can limit the number of requests that an API can handle within a certain time period. This can help prevent overloading of the API and ensure that it remains responsive for all users.

Following is a sample program on how you can use the throttle crate to rate limit an API in Rust:

```rust
use std::time::Duration;
use throttle::Throttle;

fn main() {
    // Create a throttle that allows up to 100 requests per minute.
    let throttle = Throttle::per_minute(100);

    // Wait until the throttle allows another request.
    throttle.wait();

    // Handle the request.
}
```

You can also use a monitoring tool, such as Prometheus, to track the number of requests being handled by the API and set up alerts to notify you if the request rate exceeds a certain threshold.

Another option is to use an API gateway, such as Kong or Tyk, which can handle rate limiting and other API management tasks on your behalf. These tools provide a range of features, including authentication, authorization, traffic management, and analytics, to help you monitor and control the usage of your API.

You can also use authentication and authorization mechanisms to ensure that only authorized users can access the API. One way to do this is to use an OAuth2 provider, such as Okta or Auth0, to handle the authentication and authorization process. These providers can issue access tokens to authorized users, which can then be used to access the API. You can use the oauth2 crate to validate the access tokens and ensure that only authorized users can access the API.

For example:

```rust
use oauth2::{AuthUrl, ClientId, ClientSecret, CsrfToken,
PkceCodeChallenge, RedirectUrl, TokenUrl};
use oauth2::basic::BasicClient;
use oauth2::reqwest::http_client;

fn main() {
    let client_id =
ClientId::new("YOUR_CLIENT_ID".to_string());
    let client_secret =
ClientSecret::new("YOUR_CLIENT_SECRET".to_string());
    let auth_url =
AuthUrl::new("https://YOUR_AUTH_URL".to_string());
    let token_url =
TokenUrl::new("https://YOUR_TOKEN_URL".to_string());
    let redirect_url =
RedirectUrl::new("https://YOUR_REDIRECT_URL".to_string());

    // Set up the OAuth2 client.
    let client = BasicClient::new(
        client_id,
        Some(client_secret),
        auth_url,
        Some(token_url),
```

```rust
    );

    // Generate the authorization URL.
    let (authorize_url, csrf_state) = client
        .authorize_url(CsrfToken::new_random)
        .add_scope("YOUR_SCOPE")
        .set_redirect_url(redirect_url)
        .url();

    // Redirect the user to the authorization URL.
    // ...

    // After the user grants permission, the OAuth2 provider will redirect
    // the user back to the redirect URL with an authorization code.

    // Exchange the authorization code for an access token.
    let code = "YOUR_AUTHORIZATION_CODE";
    let token = client
        .exchange_code(code)
        .add_pkce_challenge(PkceCodeChallenge::new_random)
        .request(http_client)
        .unwrap();

    // Use the access token to authenticate requests to the API.
    // ...
}
```

You can also use other authentication and authorization mechanisms, such as JSON Web Tokens (JWTs) or HTTP basic authentication, to secure your API.

CHAPTER 8: BUILDING MICROSERVICES & ARCHITECTURES

Recipe#1: Applying Fine-Grained SOA

What Is Fine-Grained SOA?

Fine-grained Service-Oriented Architecture (SOA) refers to an approach to designing and building software systems that is based on the use of small, independent units of functionality called services. These services are typically designed to be self-contained and to expose a well-defined interface that can be accessed over a network.

In a fine-grained SOA, the services are typically very small and focused on a specific aspect of the overall system functionality. This can make it easier to develop and maintain the system, as well as to scale it as needed. Fine-grained SOA is often used to build distributed systems that are made up of many different services that can be independently deployed and managed.

Features of Fine-Grained SOA

Some key characteristics of fine-grained SOA include:
- Services are designed to be self-contained and to expose a well-defined interface
- Services are typically small and focused on a specific aspect of the overall system functionality
- Services are independently deployable and manageable
- Services communicate with each other using a well-defined protocol, such as HTTP or a messaging system

Overall, the goal of fine-grained SOA is to create a flexible and scalable software architecture that can be easily maintained and modified as the needs of the system evolve.

Implement Fine-Grained SOA In Rust

Following is a sample program on how you might implement a fine-grained SOA in Rust:

First, you would define the interface for your service as a trait:

```rust
trait MyService {
    fn do_something(&self, input: String) -> Result<String,
MyError>;
}
```

Next, you would implement this trait for a struct that represents your service:

```rust
struct MyServiceImpl {
    // service-specific state and logic goes here
}

impl MyService for MyServiceImpl {
    fn do_something(&self, input: String) -> Result<String,
MyError> {
        // implement the service's functionality here
    }
}
```

You can then expose your service over a network using a library like hyper, which is a popular HTTP library for Rust:

```rust
use hyper::{Body, Request, Response, Server};
use hyper::service::{make_service_fn, service_fn};

async fn handle_request(req: Request<Body>) ->
Result<Response<Body>, hyper::Error> {
    let response_body = match (req.method(),
req.uri().path()) {
        (&hyper::Method::POST, "/do_something") => {
```

```rust
        let input = /* parse the request body as a string */;
        let result = my_service.do_something(input);
        match result {
            Ok(output) => /* create a response with the output as the body */,
            Err(error) => /* create a response with an error status code and a body describing the error */,
        }
    },
    _ => /* create a response with a "not found" status code */,
    };
    Ok(response_body)
}

#[tokio::main]
async fn main() {
    let addr = /* specify the address and port to listen on */;
    let make_service = make_service_fn(|_| async { Ok(service_fn(handle_request)) });
    let server = Server::bind(&addr).serve(make_service);
    println!("Listening on http://{}", addr);
    server.await.unwrap();
}
```

This code creates an HTTP server that listens for requests on a specific address and port. When it receives a request, it matches the method and path of the request against a set of patterns to determine how to handle it. In this case, it is looking for a POST request to the path "/do_something", and if it finds one, it invokes the do_something method on the MyService implementation. The response returned by the service is then used to create an HTTP response that is sent back to the client.

Recipe#2: Layering APIs

What Is API Layering?

API layering refers to the practice of organizing an API into a hierarchy of layers, where each layer serves a specific purpose and is isolated from the other layers. This can help to make the API more modular, scalable, and maintainable.

There are several different ways to layer an API, but a common approach is to use the following three layers:

- Presentation layer: This layer is responsible for handling the presentation of the API to the client. It typically includes the routes and controllers that handle incoming requests and send responses back to the client.
- Application layer: This layer is responsible for implementing the business logic of the API. It typically includes the services and/or models that handle the processing of data and the execution of business rules.
- Data layer: This layer is responsible for interacting with the database or other data storage systems. It typically includes the repositories and models that handle the retrieval and persistence of data.

By separating the API into these distinct layers, you can better isolate different concerns and make it easier to modify or replace one layer without affecting the others. This can make the API more flexible and easier to maintain over time.

For example, you might have a web application that uses the API to retrieve and update data stored in a database. The presentation layer would handle the incoming HTTP requests and responses, the application layer would handle the business logic of the application, and the data layer would handle the interaction with the database.

Implement API Layering

Following is a sample program on how you might implement API layering in Rust:

First, you would define the interface for each layer as a trait:

```rust
trait Presentation {
    fn handle_request(&self, req: Request) -> Result<Response, MyError>;
}

trait Application {
    fn process_data(&self, input: String) -> Result<String, MyError>;
}

trait Data {
    fn retrieve_data(&self, id: i32) -> Result<String, MyError>;
    fn update_data(&self, id: i32, data: String) -> Result<(), MyError>;
}
```

Next, you would implement these traits for structs that represent each layer:

```rust
struct PresentationImpl {
    application: Box<dyn Application>,
    // other presentation-specific state goes here
}

impl Presentation for PresentationImpl {
    fn handle_request(&self, req: Request) -> Result<Response, MyError> {
        match req.method() {
            Method::GET => {
```

```rust
                let id = /* parse the request to get the id */;
                let result = self.application.process_data(id);
                match result {
                    Ok(output) => /* create a response with the output as the body */,
                    Err(error) => /* create a response with an error status code and a body describing the error */,
                }
            },
            Method::POST => {
                let id = /* parse the request to get the id */;
                let data = /* parse the request to get the data */;
                let result = self.application.update_data(id, data);
                match result {
                    Ok(()) => /* create a response with a success status code */,
                    Err(error) => /* create a response with an error status code and a body describing the error */,
                }
            },
            _ => /* create a response with a "not found" status code */,
        }
    }
}

struct ApplicationImpl {
    data: Box<dyn Data>,
    // other application-specific state goes here
```

```rust
}

impl Application for ApplicationImpl {
    fn process_data(&self, id: i32) -> Result<String,
MyError> {
        let data = self.data.retrieve_data(id)?;
        // perform some business logic on the data
        Ok(processed_data)
    }

    fn update_data(&self, id: i32, data: String) ->
Result<(), MyError> {
        self.data.update_data(id, data)?;
        // perform some business logic after the update
        Ok(())
    }
}

struct DataImpl {
    // data-specific state goes here
}

impl Data for DataImpl {
    fn retrieve_data(&self, id: i32) -> Result<String,
MyError> {
        // retrieve the data from the database or other data
storage system
    }

    fn update_data(&self, id: i32, data: String) ->
Result<(), MyError> {
        // update the data in the database or other data
storage system
    }
```

```
}
```

Finally, you can wire everything together and start the server:

```rust
#[tokio::main]
async fn main() {
    let data = DataImpl { /* initialize data-specific state
*/ };
    let application = ApplicationImpl {
        data: Box::new(data),
        /* initialize application-specific state */
    };
    let presentation = PresentationImpl {
        application: Box::new(application),
        /* initialize presentation-specific state */
    };

    let addr = /* specify the address and port to listen on
*/;
    let make_service = make_service_fn(|_| async {
Ok(service_fn(move |req| presentation.handle_request(req)))
});
    let server = Server::bind(&addr).serve(make_service);
    println!("Listening on http://{}", addr);
    server.await.unwrap();
}
```

This code creates an HTTP server that listens for requests on a specific address and port. When it
receives a request, it passes the request to the handle_request method of the Presentation
implementation, which then invokes the appropriate methods on the Application and Data
implementations as needed. The response returned by the presentation layer is then used to create
an HTTP response that is sent back to the client.

Recipe#3: Implementing Event-Driven Communication Pattern

What Is Event-Driven Communication?

Event-driven communication is a pattern for building distributed systems where components communicate with each other by sending and receiving events. An event is a message that indicates that something has happened, and it typically includes data that describes the event in more detail.

In an event-driven system, components are designed to be independent and to communicate asynchronously with each other. This means that when one component sends an event to another component, it does not wait for a response. Instead, the receiving component processes the event and may send one or more additional events in response. This can help to make the system more scalable and resilient, as components can operate independently and do not have to block on each other's responses.

There are several different ways to implement event-driven communication, but some common approaches include:
- Using a message queue or messaging system, such as Apache Kafka or RabbitMQ, to send and receive events
- Using a publish/subscribe model, where components can publish events to a central event bus and other components can subscribe to receive events that match their interests
- Using a webhook model, where components can register their interest in certain types of events and receive a HTTP callback when those events occur

Overall, event-driven communication can be a useful pattern for building distributed systems that need to be highly scalable and responsive. It can also make it easier to build systems that are modular and flexible, as components can be added or removed without affecting the overall functionality of the system.

Implementing Event-Driven Communication Pattern In Rust

Following is a sample program on how you might implement event-driven communication in Rust using a message queue:

First, you would define the interface for your event types as a trait:

```rust
trait Event {
    fn name(&self) -> &str;
}


#[derive(Debug, Serialize, Deserialize)]
struct MyEvent {
    // event-specific fields go here
}


impl Event for MyEvent {
    fn name(&self) -> &str {
        "my_event"
    }
}
```

Next, you would set up a connection to your message queue and define a function for sending events:

```rust
use amqp::{Session, Options, Channel, Basic, Table, Protocol};
use serde::Serialize;

fn send_event<T>(channel: &Channel, event: &T) -> Result<(), MyError>
    where T: Event + Serialize
{
```

```
    let payload = bincode::serialize(event)?;
    let properties = BasicProperties {
        content_type: "application/octet-stream".into(),
        ..Default::default()
    };
    channel.basic_publish("",  event.name(),  false,  false,
properties, payload)?;
    Ok(())
}
```

You can then use this function to send events as needed:

```
let session = Session::new(Options {
    host: "localhost".into(),
    port: 5672,
    vhost: "/".into(),
    login: "guest".into(),
    password: "guest".into(),
    ..Default::default()
})?;

let channel = session.open_channel(1)?;
let event = MyEvent { /* initialize event fields */ };
send_event(&channel, &event)?;
```

To receive events, you can set up a consumer using the basic_consume method of the Channel
struct:

```
use amqp::{BasicConsumeOptions, Consumer, BasicProperties};
use serde::Deserialize;

fn receive_event<T>(channel: &Channel) -> Result<T, MyError>
    where T: Event + Deserialize<'static>
```

```
{
    let consumer = channel.basic_consume(T::name(), "",
BasicConsumeOptions::default(), Table::new())?;
    let delivery = consumer.recv().await?;
    let payload = delivery.data;
    let event = bincode::deserialize(&payload)?;
    Ok(event)
}
```

You can then use this function to receive events as needed:

```
let event = receive_event::<MyEvent>(&channel).await?;
// process the event
```

Recipe#4: Programming Middlewares

Understanding Need of Middlewares

In Rust programs, middlewares are functions or structs that are used to intercept and modify requests and responses as they pass through an HTTP server or client. Middlewares are often used to add functionality to an HTTP server or client, such as logging, authentication, or error handling.

To use middlewares in Rust, you typically define a struct or function that implements a specific trait or interface. This trait or interface will usually have a method that takes a Request and Response as arguments, and returns a new Response. This method is called to modify the request or response as needed before it is passed on to the next middleware or to the final handler.

Programming Middlewares for Logging Service

Following is a sample program of a simple middleware in Rust that logs the request and response:

```rust
use hyper::{Request, Response, Body};
use hyper::service::{Service, MakeService};

struct LogMiddleware<S> {
    service: S,
}

impl<S> Service for LogMiddleware<S>
    where S: Service<Request = Request<Body>>,
          S::Response: Into<Response<Body>>,
{
    type Request = S::Request;
    type Response = S::Response;
    type Error = S::Error;
    type Future = S::Future;

    fn poll_ready(&mut self, cx: &mut Context) -> Poll<Result<(), Self::Error>> {
        self.service.poll_ready(cx)
    }

    fn call(&mut self, req: Request<Body>) -> Self::Future {
        println!("Received request: {:?}", req);
        let fut = self.service.call(req);
        async move {
            let res = fut.await?;
            println!("Sending response: {:?}", res);
            Ok(res)
        }
    }
}
```

```rust
impl<S> LogMiddleware<S> {
    fn new(service: S) -> Self {
        LogMiddleware { service }
    }
}

impl<S> MakeService for LogMiddleware<S>
    where S: Service<Request = Request<Body>>,
          S::Response: Into<Response<Body>>,
{
    type Request = S::Request;
    type Response = S::Response;
    type Error = S::Error;
    type Service = Self;
    type MakeError = ();
    type        Future        =        FutureResult<Self::Service,
Self::MakeError>;

    fn make_service(&self, _: &AddrStream) -> Self::Future {

future::ok(LogMiddleware::new(self.service.clone()))
    }
}
```

This code defines a LogMiddleware struct that wraps a service and logs the request and response as they pass through the middleware. It implements the Service trait from the hyper library, which allows it to be used as a handler in an HTTP server. It also implements the MakeService trait, which allows it to be used to create a new instance of the middleware for each incoming connection.

To use this middleware, you can wrap your service in a LogMiddleware instance and pass it to an HTTP server:

```rust
let service = MyService { /* initialize service state */ };
```

```
let middleware = LogMiddleware::new(service);
let server = Server::bind(&addr).serve(middleware);
```

Stacking Multiple Middlewares

To stack multiple middlewares in an application, you can define a struct or function for each middleware that implements the appropriate trait or interface. Then, you can use these structs or functions to wrap your service in a series of middlewares, with the innermost middleware being the one closest to the service itself.

Following is a sample program on how you might stack multiple middlewares in an application:

```
use hyper::{Request, Response, Body};
use hyper::service::{Service, MakeService};

struct LogMiddleware<S> {
    service: S,
}

impl<S> Service for LogMiddleware<S>
    where S: Service<Request = Request<Body>>,
        S::Response: Into<Response<Body>>,
{
    type Request = S::Request;
    type Response = S::Response;
    type Error = S::Error;
    type Future = S::Future;

    fn poll_ready(&mut self, cx: &mut Context) ->
Poll<Result<(), Self::Error>> {
        self.service.poll_ready(cx)
    }
```

```rust
    fn call(&mut self, req: Request<Body>) -> Self::Future {
        println!("Received request: {:?}", req);
        let fut = self.service.call(req);
        async move {
            let res = fut.await?;
            println!("Sending response: {:?}", res);
            Ok(res)
        }
    }
}

impl<S> LogMiddleware<S> {
    fn new(service: S) -> Self {
        LogMiddleware { service }
    }
}

impl<S> MakeService for LogMiddleware<S>
    where S: Service<Request = Request<Body>>,
        S::Response: Into<Response<Body>>,
{
    type Request = S::Request;
    type Response = S::Response;
    type Error = S::Error;
    type Service = Self;
    type MakeError = ();
    type       Future       =       FutureResult<Self::Service,
Self::MakeError>

let service = MyService { /* initialize service state */ };

// Wrap the service in a chain of middlewares
let middleware1 = LogMiddleware::new(service);
let                     middleware2                     =
```

```
AuthenticationMiddleware::new(middleware1);
let middleware3 = ErrorHandlingMiddleware::new(middleware2);

let server = Server::bind(&addr).serve(middleware3);
```

In this example, the MyService struct represents the innermost service that handles the actual business logic of the application. The LogMiddleware, AuthenticationMiddleware, and ErrorHandlingMiddleware structs represent the middlewares that are stacked around the service.

When a request is received by the server, it is passed to the outermost middleware (ErrorHandlingMiddleware in this example). The middleware can modify the request or response as needed before passing it on to the next middleware in the chain (AuthenticationMiddleware in this example). This process continues until the request reaches the innermost middleware (LogMiddleware in this example), which passes the request to the service for processing. The response from the service is then passed back through the middlewares in reverse order, with each middleware modifying the response as needed before passing it on to the next middleware. Finally, the modified response is returned to the client.

Recipe#5: End-To-End API Testing

What Is API Testing?

API testing is a type of software testing that focuses on testing the interfaces of application programming interfaces (APIs). APIs are sets of protocols, routines, and tools for building software and applications, and they provide a way for different components of a system to communicate with each other.

API testing involves testing the functionality, reliability, and performance of an API to ensure that it meets the requirements of the system and the needs of the users. This can include testing the input and output of the API, testing the error handling and validation of the API, and testing the security of the API.

API testing can be performed manually, using tools like curl or Postman, or it can be automated using a testing framework or library. Automated API testing can help to ensure that an API is tested consistently and thoroughly, and it can save time and effort by eliminating the need to manually test the API repeatedly.

Overall, API testing is an important part of the software development process, as it helps to ensure that the APIs of a system are reliable, stable, and secure.

Running End-To-End API Testing In Rust -

Following is a sample program on how you might perform end-to-end API testing in Rust:

First, you would define a function that sends an HTTP request to the API and returns the response:

```rust
use hyper::{Client, Uri};
use hyper_tls::HttpsConnector;
use tokio::runtime::Runtime;

async fn send_request(url: &str) -> Result<String, MyError>
{
    let https = HttpsConnector::new();
    let client = Client::builder().build::<_,
hyper::Body>(https);
    let uri: Uri = url.parse()?;
    let res = client.get(uri).await?;
    let body = 
hyper::body::to_bytes(res.into_body()).await?;
    Ok(String::from_utf8(body.to_vec())?)
}
```

Next, you would define a test function that sends a request to the API and verifies the response:

```
#[test]
fn test_api() {
    let mut rt = Runtime::new().unwrap();
    let                             res                         =
rt.block_on(send_request("https://example.com/api/endpoint"
));
    assert!(res.is_ok());
    let res = res.unwrap();
    assert_eq!(res, "expected response");
}
```

This test function uses the Runtime from the tokio library to execute the asynchronous send_request function synchronously. It then verifies that the response is successful and that it matches the expected value.

You can then run this test function as part of your testing suite to ensure that the API is functioning correctly. You can also define additional test functions to test different aspects of the API, such as different input values or error conditions.

Recipe#6: Splitting Monoliths with Strangler Fig Pattern

What Is Splitting Monoliths?

Splitting monoliths refers to the process of breaking down a large, monolithic software system into smaller, more modular components. This can be done for a variety of reasons, including to improve the scalability, maintainability, and flexibility of the system.

A monolithic system is one in which all of the components of the system are tightly coupled and depend on each other, making it difficult to change or modify one part of the system without affecting the rest of the system. In contrast, a modular system is one in which the components are more independent and can be changed or modified more easily without affecting the rest of the system.

Benefit of Splitting Monoliths

Splitting a monolithic system into smaller, more modular components can have several benefits, including:

- Improved scalability: Modular systems can be more easily scaled up or down, as each component can be independently scaled to meet the needs of the system.
- Improved maintainability: Modular systems are generally easier to maintain and update, as changes to one component are less likely to affect the rest of the system.
- Improved flexibility: Modular systems are generally more flexible and adaptable, as they can be more easily modified or replaced to meet changing requirements or needs.
- Improved reliability: Modular systems are often more reliable, as they are less likely to be affected by changes to other components of the system.

Overall, splitting monoliths can help to improve the scalability, maintainability, flexibility, and reliability of a software system, making it easier to develop, maintain, and evolve over time.

Strangler Fig Pattern Explained!

The Strangler Fig Pattern is a design pattern that is used to incrementally replace a monolithic system with a set of microservices. It is named after the strangler fig tree, which is a type of plant that grows around and eventually strangles its host tree, eventually replacing it with a new tree.

The Strangler Fig Pattern involves building a new system around the existing monolithic system, with the new system handling some of the functionality of the monolithic system and the monolithic system handling the rest. Over time, more and more functionality is moved from the monolithic system to the new system, until eventually the monolithic system is completely replaced.

The Strangler Fig Pattern has several benefits, including:

- Incremental replacement: The Strangler Fig Pattern allows you to replace the monolithic system incrementally, rather than all at once, which can reduce the risk and complexity of the migration.
- Continuous delivery: The Strangler Fig Pattern allows you to continuously deliver new functionality to users while the migration is ongoing, rather than having to wait until the entire migration is complete.
- Reduced risk: The Strangler Fig Pattern reduces the risk of the migration, as the monolithic system remains in place and can be used as a fallback if there are any issues with the new system.

Overall, the Strangler Fig Pattern is a useful approach for migrating from a monolithic system to a set of microservices, as it allows you to replace the monolithic system incrementally and continuously deliver new functionality to users while the migration is ongoing.

Implementing The Strangler Fig Pattern to Split Monoliths

Following is a sample program on how you might implement the Strangler Fig Pattern in Rust to split a monolithic system into microservices:

First, you would define the API for the new microservice:

```rust
use actix_web::{web, App, HttpServer};

fn main() -> std::io::Result<()> {
    HttpServer::new(|| {
        App::new()
            .route("/api/endpoint",
web::get().to(api_handler))
    })
    .bind("127.0.0.1:8080")?
```

```
        .run()
}

async fn api_handler() -> String {
    // handle API request and return response
}
```

Next, you would modify the monolithic system to call the new microservice when needed:

```
use reqwest::Client;

fn main() {
    let client = Client::new();
    let                             res                         =
client.get("http://localhost:8080/api/endpoint").send().unw
rap();
    let body = res.text().unwrap();
    println!("{}", body);
}
```

This modified monolithic system now calls the new microservice to handle some of its functionality, while the rest of the functionality is still handled by the monolithic system.

Over time, you can continue to move more and more functionality from the monolithic system to the new microservice, until eventually the monolithic system is completely replaced by the microservice.

Recipe#7: Autoscaling Rust Programs

Rust Libraries for Autoscaling Applications

There are several libraries and frameworks in Rust that you can use to implement autoscaling in your Rust programs. Some popular options include:

- tokio: The tokio library is a Rust library for building asynchronous, concurrent, and scalable applications. It provides a lightweight, fast, and reliable runtime for building high-performance applications.
- hyper: The hyper library is a Rust library for building HTTP clients and servers. It provides a high-level API for making HTTP requests and handling HTTP responses, and it is built on top of the tokio library.
- actix-web: The actix-web library is a Rust library for building web applications and services. It provides a high-level API for building web servers, routing requests, and handling responses, and it is built on top of the actix library.
- wasm-bindgen: The wasm-bindgen library is a Rust library for building WebAssembly (WASM) modules and applications. It provides a high-level API for building WASM modules and interacting with them from JavaScript, and it is built on top of the wasm-bindgen-futures library.

These are just a few examples of libraries and frameworks that you can use to implement autoscaling in Rust programs.

Autoscaling Rust Applications with Tokio

Following is a sample program on how you might use the tokio library to autoscale a Rust application:

First, you would define a function that performs the work you want to scale:

```rust
use tokio::task;

async fn work() {
```

```
    // perform work here
}

#[tokio::main]
async fn main() {
    for _ in 0..10 {
        let task = task::spawn(work());
        task.await.unwrap();
    }
}
```

In this example, the work function performs some work asynchronously, and the main function spawns 10 tasks to run the work concurrently.

To autoscale this application, you can use the num_cpus function from the num_cpus crate to determine the number of CPUs available on the system and use that to determine the number of tasks to spawn:

```
use num_cpus;
use tokio::task;

async fn work() {
    // perform work here
}

#[tokio::main]
async fn main() {
    let num_cpus = num_cpus::get();
    for _ in 0..num_cpus {
        let task = task::spawn(work());
        task.await.unwrap();
    }
}
```

This modified version of the application will spawn one task for each CPU on the system, allowing the work to be scaled up or down depending on the resources available on the system.

CHAPTER 9: WORKING AROUND CI/CD

Continuous integration (CI) and continuous delivery (CD) are software development practices that aim to reduce the time it takes to develop and deliver software by automating the build, test, and deployment process.

In the context of Rust, CI/CD typically involves setting up a pipeline that automatically builds and tests a Rust project whenever new code is pushed to a version control repository (such as Git). If the build and tests are successful, the pipeline can then automatically deploy the new code to a staging or production environment, making it available to users.

Kubernetes is a container orchestration platform that can be used to deploy, scale, and manage containerized applications. It can be integrated into a CI/CD pipeline to automate the deployment of Rust applications to a Kubernetes cluster.

Recipe#1: Setting Up a Version Control Repository

Choosing Version Control System

To set up a version control repository for a Rust project, you will need to choose a version control system and then initialize the repository for your project.

One popular option for version control in Rust is Git, which is a distributed version control system that allows developers to track changes to their code over time and collaborate with others.

Setting Up Git Repo

To set up a Git repository for your Rust project, follow these steps:

Install Git on your computer if it is not already installed. You can download the latest version of Git from the official website (https://git-scm.com/) or use a package manager to install it.

Navigate to the directory that contains your Rust project.

Initialize a new Git repository by running the following command:

```
git init
```

Add all of the files in your Rust project to the Git repository by running the following command:

```
git add .
```

Commit the added files to the repository by running the following command:

```
git commit -m "Initial commit"
```

If you want to host your repository online (For example, on GitHub), you will need to create a new repository on the hosting service and then add it as a remote for your local repository. To do this, run the following command, replacing <remote-repository-url> with the URL of your online repository:

```
git remote add origin <remote-repository-url>
```

To push your local repository to the online repository, run the following command:

```
git push -u origin master
```

This will create a new Git repository for your Rust project and add all of the files in the project to it. You can then use Git to track changes to your code and collaborate with other developers.

Branching: Git allows you to create multiple branches of your codebase, which can be used to develop new features or fix bugs without affecting the main codebase (the "master" branch). You can create a new branch by running the following command:

```
git branch <branch-name>
```

You can switch to a different branch by running the following command:

```
git checkout <branch-name>
```

Merging: When you are ready to incorporate changes from one branch into another, you can use the git merge command to merge the changes from the source branch into the target branch. For example, to merge changes from a branch named "feature" into the master branch, you would run the following command:

```
git checkout master
git merge feature
```

Stashing: Sometimes, you may want to temporarily store changes that you have made to your codebase without committing them to the repository. You can use the git stash command to do this. When you are ready to reapply the stashed changes, you can use the git stash apply command.

Reverting: If you make a mistake or want to undo a change that you have made, you can use the git revert command to revert the change. This creates a new commit that undoes the changes made in the specified commit.

Tagging: You can use Git tags to mark specific commits in your repository as being important. This can be useful for marking releases or other significant milestones in your project's development. You can create a new tag by running the following command:

```
git tag <tag-name>
```

You can push the tags to a remote repository using the git push command with the --tags option:

```
git push --tags
```

Configuration: Git allows you to customize various aspects of your repository and workflow using configuration files. For example, you can set your name and email address (which will be associated with your commits) by running the following commands:

```
git config --global user.name "Your Name"
git config --global user.email "your@email.com"
```

You can also set up aliases for Git commands and customize the behavior of various Git features using the configuration files.

Recipe#2: Configuring a CI/CD Pipeline

Understanding Continuous Integration and Continuous Delivery

A CI/CD (Continuous Integration / Continuous Delivery) pipeline is a set of automated processes that are used to build, test, and deploy software applications. The goal of a CI/CD pipeline is to reduce the time it takes to develop and deliver software by automating various parts of the development and deployment process.

To configure a CI/CD pipeline in Rust, you will need to choose a CI/CD platform and set up the necessary configuration files and scripts to define the pipeline. Some popular CI/CD platforms for Rust include GitHub Actions, CircleCI, and Jenkins.

Configuring CI/CD Pipeline Using GitHub Actions

Following is a sample program on how you might configure a CI/CD pipeline for a Rust project using GitHub Actions:

- Set up a version control repository for your Rust project (e.g. using Git).
- Create a new repository on GitHub and push your local repository to it.
- In the repository on GitHub, go to the Actions tab and click the "Set up a workflow yourself" button.
- Create a new file named main.yml in the .github/workflows directory. This file will contain the configuration for your CI/CD pipeline.
- In the main.yml file, define the triggers for your pipeline. For example, you might want the pipeline to run whenever new code is pushed to the repository or when a pull request is opened. You can use the following syntax to define a trigger:

```
on:
  push:
    branches:
      - master
```

- Define the jobs that your pipeline will run. A job consists of a series of steps that are executed in order. You can define multiple jobs in your pipeline and specify dependencies between them. For example, you might have a job to build and test your Rust project, and another job to deploy the built artifacts to a staging environment. Following is a sample program on how you might define a job to build and test your Rust project:

```
jobs:
  build:
    runs-on: ubuntu-latest
    steps:
    - uses: actions/checkout@v2
    - name: Install Rust
      uses: actions-rs/toolchain@v1
      with:
        toolchain: stable
```

```
- name: Build and test project
  run: cargo build && cargo test
```

If you want to deploy your Rust project to a staging or production environment, you can define additional jobs in your pipeline to handle the deployment. For example, you might use the scp command to copy the built artifacts to a staging server, or use a tool like Terraform to provision infrastructure and deploy the project to a cloud platform.

Recipe#3: Customizing CI/CD Pipeline

Steps to Customize CI/CD

Following are some helpful practical steps that you can follow to customize and extend an existing CI/CD pipeline for a Rust project:

- Identify the tasks or steps that you want to add to your pipeline. For example, you might want to add additional tests, deploy to multiple environments, or integrate with an external service.
- Determine the appropriate place in the pipeline to add the new tasks or steps. For example, you might want to run the new tasks after the existing build and test steps, or as part of a separate job.
- Write the necessary configuration files and scripts to define the new tasks or steps. For example, you might use a shell script to run additional tests, or use a tool like Terraform to provision infrastructure.
- Test the new tasks or steps locally to ensure that they are working as expected.
- Commit the changes to your version control repository and push them to the remote repository.
- Observe the pipeline as it runs to ensure that the new tasks or steps are being executed correctly.
- If necessary, debug any issues that arise and make any necessary adjustments to the

configuration or scripts.

- Repeat the process as needed to add additional tasks or steps to your pipeline.
- Remember to test your changes thoroughly before deploying them to production, and consider using feature flags or other techniques to roll out changes incrementally if necessary.

Overall, the key to customizing and extending a CI/CD pipeline is to carefully plan and test your changes to ensure that they are working as expected and do not cause disruptions to the pipeline.

Recipe#4: Integrating CI/CD Pipeline with Databases and Message Queue

Procedure to Integrate CI/CD Pipeline

Following are the steps to integrate a CI/CD pipeline for a Rust project with a database and message queue:

- First, you will need to set up a database and message queue to use with your Rust project. For example, you might use a MySQL database and a RabbitMQ message queue.
- Next, you will need to configure your Rust project to connect to the database and message queue. This typically involves installing the necessary libraries and dependencies and writing code to establish the connections and perform operations such as querying the database or sending messages to the message queue.
- Once you have your Rust project configured to use the database and message queue, you can integrate the database and message queue into your CI/CD pipeline. This will typically involve adding additional jobs or steps to the pipeline to perform tasks such as provisioning the database and message queue, running database migrations, or sending messages to the message queue.

Use of MySQL, amiquip and RabbitMQ

Following is a sample program on how you might use the Rust MySQL library and the Rust amiquip library to connect to a MySQL database and send a message to a RabbitMQ message queue in a CI/CD pipeline job:

```
jobs:
  database:
    runs-on: ubuntu-latest
    steps:
    - name: Connect to MySQL database
      run: |
        # Install the MySQL client library
        cargo install mysql-client
        # Connect to the MySQL database and run a query
        mysql --host=<database-host> --user=<database-user>
--password=<database-password> --execute="SELECT * FROM
users"
  message-queue:
    runs-on: ubuntu-latest
    steps:
    - name: Send message to RabbitMQ message queue
      run: |
        # Install the amiquip library
        cargo install amiquip
        # Send a message to the message queue
        amqp-send --url=amqp://<message-queue-host> --
exchange=<exchange-name> --routing-key=<routing-key> --
body="Hello, world!"
```

This is just a basic example of how you might integrate a database and message queue into a CI/CD pipeline for a Rust project. There are many other options and features that you can use to customize and extend the integration to meet the needs of your project.

Overall, the goal of integrating a database and message queue into a CI/CD pipeline is to automate tasks such as provisioning infrastructure, running database migrations, and sending messages, which can help to streamline the development and deployment process for your Rust project.

Recipe#5: Setting Up Docker Hub Container Registry

What Is Docker Hub?

Docker Hub is a cloud-based registry service for Docker images. It allows you to store, manage, and share Docker images with others. Docker Hub includes features such as image storage, image building, and image distribution.

Understanding Container Registry

A container registry is a repository for storing and distributing container images. Docker Hub is one example of a container registry, but there are many other options available as well, such as Google Container Registry, Azure Container Registry, and Amazon Elastic Container Registry.

Steps to Setup Container Registry

In the context of a CI/CD pipeline for a Rust project, you might use a container registry to store the built Rust containers that are generated by the pipeline. This can make it easier to deploy the containers to different environments, such as staging or production.

To use a container registry with a Rust project, you will typically need to perform the following steps:

- Create an account on the container registry service and authenticate with it.
- Build a Docker image for your Rust project using the Dockerfile and other necessary files.
- Tag the Docker image with the desired repository and tag names.
- Push the Docker image to the container registry using the docker push command.

For example, to push a Docker image for a Rust project to Docker Hub, you might run the following commands:

```
# Build the Docker image
docker build -t my-rust-project .

# Tag the Docker image
docker tag my-rust-project <docker-hub-username>/my-rust-project:latest

# Push the Docker image to Docker Hub
docker push <docker-hub-username>/my-rust-project:latest
```

The above are just the basic steps for using a container registry with a Rust project

Establishing Container Registry On Docker Hub

To set up a Docker Hub container registry for a Rust project, you can follow these steps:

- Create an account on Docker Hub and log in.
- Create a new repository on Docker Hub for your Rust project.
- Create a Dockerfile for your Rust project. The Dockerfile should specify the steps needed to build the Rust project and package it in a Docker container.
- Build the Docker image for your Rust project using the Dockerfile and other necessary files. You can do this using the docker build command:

```
docker build -t my-rust-project
```

- Tag the Docker image with the repository and tag names that you specified on Docker Hub. You can do this using the docker tag command:

```
docker tag my-rust-project <docker-hub-username>/my-rust-project:latest
```

- Push the Docker image to Docker Hub using the docker push command:

```
docker push <docker-hub-username>/my-rust-project:latest
```

- Set up automation in your CI/CD pipeline to build and push the Docker image to Docker Hub on a regular basis.

By following these steps, you can set up a Docker Hub container registry for a Rust project and make it easier to deploy your Rust project to different environments.

CHAPTER 10: WORKING AROUND KUBERNETES

Recipe#1: Setting Up a Kubernetes Cluster On-Premises

What Is Cluster?

A cluster refers to a group of interconnected computers that work together to perform a common task. In the context of Kubernetes, a cluster refers to a group of nodes (physical or virtual machines) that are running the Kubernetes software and are connected to each other.

What Is Kubernetes Cluster?

Kubernetes is an open-source container orchestration system that allows you to deploy, scale, and manage containerized applications. One of the key features of Kubernetes is its ability to create and manage clusters of nodes that can run containerized applications.

Establishing Kubernetes Cluster On-Premises

To set up a Kubernetes cluster on-premises (that is, on your own infrastructure rather than in the cloud), you will need to perform the following steps:

- Install the necessary software and dependencies on the nodes that will be part of the cluster. This will typically involve installing the Kubernetes software, as well as a container runtime such as Docker.
- Configure the nodes to communicate with each other and form a cluster. This will typically involve setting up a network and configuring the nodes to join the cluster.
- Set up additional components or tools to manage and monitor the cluster, such as a load balancer or monitoring system.

Following is a sample program on how you might set up a Kubernetes cluster on-premises using the kubeadm tool:

Install the necessary software and dependencies on the nodes that will be part of the cluster. This will typically involve installing the Kubernetes software, as well as a container runtime such as Docker:

```
# Install the Kubernetes software
apt-get update && apt-get install -y kubeadm

# Install Docker
apt-get update && apt-get install -y docker.io
```

Configure the nodes to communicate with each other and form a cluster. This will typically involve setting up a network and configuring the nodes to join the cluster:

```
# Set up a network for the cluster
kubeadm init --pod-network-cidr=10.244.0.0/16

# Copy the configuration files to the home directory
mkdir -p $HOME/.kube
cp -i /etc/kubernetes/admin.conf $HOME/.kube/config

# Join the nodes to the cluster
kubeadm join <cluster-ip>:<cluster-port> --token <token> --
discovery-token-ca-cert-hash sha256:<hash>
```

Recipe#2: Setting Up a Kubernetes Cluster On AWS

Using AWS CLI and kubeadm for Setting Up Kubernetes Cluster

Following is a sample program on how you might set up a Kubernetes cluster on the Amazon Web Services (AWS) platform using the AWS Command Line Interface (CLI) and the kubeadm tool:

- Install the AWS CLI on your local machine and configure it with your AWS access keys.

```
# Install the AWS CLI
pip install awscli

# Configure the AWS CLI
aws configure
```

- Set up an IAM user with the necessary permissions to create and manage resources on AWS. You will need to specify the permissions that the user should have, such as the ability to create EC2 instances and manage VPCs.

```
# Create the IAM policy
{
  "Version": "2012-10-17",
  "Statement": [
    {
      "Effect": "Allow",
      "Action": "ec2:*",
      "Resource": "*"
    },
    {
      "Effect": "Allow",
```

```
      "Action": "iam:*",
      "Resource": "*"
    },
    {
      "Effect": "Allow",
      "Action": "elasticloadbalancing:*",
      "Resource": "*"
    }
  ]
}

# Create the IAM user
aws iam create-user --user-name <user-name>

# Attach the IAM policy to the IAM user
aws iam attach-user-policy --policy-arn <policy-arn> --user-
name <user-name>
```

- Create a VPC (Virtual Private Cloud) on AWS. This will provide the networking infrastructure for your Kubernetes cluster.

```
# Create the VPC
aws ec2 create-vpc --cidr-block <cidr-block>

# Create a subnet
aws ec2 create-subnet --vpc-id <vpc-id> --cidr-block <cidr-
block>

# Create an internet gateway
aws ec2 create-internet-gateway

# Attach the internet gateway to the VPC
aws ec2 attach-internet-gateway --vpc-id <vpc-id> --internet-
gateway-id <internet-gateway-id>
```

```
# Create a route table
aws ec2 create-route-table --v
```

- Create an EC2 key pair. This will allow you to securely SSH into the EC2 instances that will be part of your Kubernetes cluster.

```
# Create the EC2 key pair
aws ec2 create-key-pair --key-name <key-name> --query
'KeyMaterial' --output text > <key-name>.pem

# Change the permissions on the key pair file
chmod 400 <key-name>.pem
```

- Launch an EC2 instance to use as the master node for your Kubernetes cluster. You will need to specify the AMI (Amazon Machine Image) to use, as well as the instance type and other settings.

```
# Launch the EC2 instance
aws ec2 run-instances \
  --image-id <ami-id> \
  --instance-type <instance-type> \
  --key-name <key-name> \
  --subnet-id <subnet-id> \
  --security-group-ids <security-group-id>

# Wait for the EC2 instance to become available
aws ec2 wait instance-running --instance-ids <instance-id>
```

- Set up the master node to act as the control plane for your Kubernetes cluster. This will typically involve initializing the cluster using the kubeadm tool and configuring the nodes to join the cluster.

```
# Install the Kubernetes software
apt-get update && apt-get install -y kubeadm

# Install Docker
apt-get update && apt-get install -y docker.io

# Initialize the cluster using kubeadm
kubeadm init --pod-network-cidr=10.244.0.0/16

# Copy the configuration files to the home directory
mkdir -p $HOME/.kube
cp -i /etc/kubernetes/admin.conf $HOME/.kube/config
```

- Launch additional EC2 instances to use as worker nodes for your Kubernetes cluster. You will need to specify the AMI, instance type, and other settings as before.

```
# Launch the EC2 instances
aws ec2 run-instances \
  --image-id <ami-id> \
  --instance-type <instance-type> \
  --key-name <
```

By following these steps, you can set up a Kubernetes cluster on the AWS platform using the AWS CLI and the kubeadm tool. You can then deploy containerized applications to the cluster using the Kubernetes software.

Recipe#3: Setting Up a Kubernetes Cluster On Google Cloud

Using gcloud and kubeadm to Setup Kubernetes Cluster

Following is a sample program on how you might set up a Kubernetes cluster on the Google Cloud Platform (GCP) using the gcloud command line tool and the kubeadm tool:

- Install the gcloud command line tool on your local machine and configure it with your GCP account and project.

```
# Install the gcloud command line tool
curl https://sdk.cloud.google.com | bash

# Configure the gcloud CLI
gcloud init
```

- Create a Compute Engine network and a firewall rule to allow traffic to the Kubernetes cluster.

```
# Create the network
gcloud compute networks create <network-name> --subnet-mode
custom

# Create a subnet
gcloud compute networks subnets create <subnet-name> --
network <network-name> --range <cidr-range>

# Create a firewall rule to allow traffic to the cluster
gcloud compute firewall-rules create <firewall-rule-name> --
allow tcp:6443,tcp:2379-2380,tcp:10250-10252,tcp:10255
```

- Create a Compute Engine instance to use as the master node for your Kubernetes cluster. You will need to specify the image to use, as well as the instance type and other settings.

```
# Create the Compute Engine instance
gcloud compute instances create <instance-name> \
  --image-family <image-family> \
  --image-project <image-project> \
  --machine-type <machine-type> \
  --subnet <subnet-name>
```

- Install the necessary software and dependencies on the master node. This will typically involve installing the Kubernetes software, as well as a container runtime such as Docker.

```
# Update the package manager and install the Kubernetes
software
apt-get update && apt-get install -y kubeadm

# Install Docker
apt-get update && apt-get install -y docker.io
```

- Set up the master node to act as the control plane for your Kubernetes cluster. This will typically involve initializing the cluster using the kubeadm tool and configuring the nodes to join the cluster.

```
# Initialize the cluster using kubeadm
kubeadm init --pod-network-cidr=10.244.0.0/16

# Copy the configuration files to the home directory
mkdir -p $HOME/.kube
cp -i /etc/kubernetes/admin.conf $HOME/.kube/config
```

- Join the worker nodes to the cluster using the kubeadm tool.

```
# Join the worker nodes to the cluster
kubeadm   join   <master-node-ip>:6443   --token   <token>   --
discovery-token-ca-cert-hash <hash>
```

By following these steps, you can set up a Kubernetes cluster on the GCP platform using the gcloud command line tool and the kubeadm tool. You can then deploy containerized applications to the cluster using the Kubernetes software.

Recipe#4: Setting Up a Kubernetes Cluster On Microsoft Azure

Using Azure CLI and kubeadm for Kubernetes Cluster

Following is a sample program on how you might set up a Kubernetes cluster on the Microsoft Azure platform using the Azure CLI and the kubeadm tool:

- Install the Azure CLI on your local machine and log in to your Azure account.

```
# Install the Azure CLI
curl -sL https://aka.ms/InstallAzureCLIDeb | sudo bash

# Log in to your Azure account
az login
Create  a  resource  group  to  hold  the  resources  for  your
Kubernetes cluster.

# Create the resource group
az   group   create   --name   <resource-group-name>   --location
```

```
<location>
```

- Create a virtual network and a subnet to provide the networking infrastructure for your Kubernetes cluster.

```
# Create the virtual network
az network vnet create --name <vnet-name> --resource-group
<resource-group-name> --address-prefixes <address-prefixes>
--subnet-name <subnet-name> --subnet-prefix <subnet-prefix>

# Create a network security group
az network nsg create --name <nsg-name> --resource-group
<resource-group-name>

# Create a security rule to allow traffic to the cluster
az network nsg rule create --nsg-name <nsg-name> --name
<rule-name> --protocol tcp --destination-port-range 6443 --
access allow
```

- Create a virtual machine to use as the master node for your Kubernetes cluster. You will need to specify the image to use, as well as the instance type and other settings.

```
# Create the virtual machine
az vm create --name <vm-name> --resource-group <resource-
group-name> --image <image> --size <size> --vnet-name <vnet-
name> --subnet <subnet-name> --nsg <nsg-name>
```

- Install the necessary software and dependencies on the master node. This will typically involve installing the Kubernetes software, as well as a container runtime such as Docker.

```
# Update the package manager and install the Kubernetes
software
```

```
apt-get update && apt-get install -y kubeadm

# Install Docker
apt-get update && apt-get install -y docker.io
```

- Set up the master node to act as the control plane for your Kubernetes cluster. This will typically involve initializing the cluster using the kubeadm tool and configuring the nodes to join the cluster.

```
# Initialize the cluster using kubeadm
kubeadm init --pod-network-cidr=10.244.0.0/16

# Copy the configuration files to the home directory
mkdir -p $HOME
```

- Join the worker nodes to the cluster using the kubeadm tool.

```
# Join the worker nodes to the cluster
kubeadm join <master-node-ip>:6443 --token <token> --discovery-token-ca-cert-hash <hash>
```

By following these steps, you can set up a Kubernetes cluster on the Azure platform using the Azure CLI and the kubeadm tool. You can then deploy containerized applications to the cluster using the Kubernetes software.

Recipe#5: Testing The Cluster Setup Across AWS, GCP and Azure

Procedure to Test the Kubernetes Cluster

Following are some helpful steps you can follow to test the setup of your Kubernetes cluster across the Amazon Web Services (AWS), Google Cloud Platform (GCP), and Microsoft Azure platforms:

- Verify that the cluster is running and all nodes are healthy. You can use the kubectl command line tool to check the status of the cluster and its nodes.

```
# Check the status of the cluster
kubectl get nodes

# Check the status of the pods in the cluster
kubectl get pods --all-namespaces
```

- Deploy a test application to the cluster. You can use the kubectl tool to deploy a simple test application to the cluster, such as a simple web server or a database.

```
# Deploy a test application to the cluster
kubectl apply -f <test-application-manifest.yaml>
```

- Verify that the test application is running and can be accessed from outside the cluster. You can use the kubectl tool to check the status of the test application, as well as access it from your local machine or another device.

```
# Check the status of the test application
kubectl get pods --all-namespaces
```

```
# Access the test application from your local machine
curl <test-application-url>
```

- Test the cluster's scalability. You can use the kubectl tool to scale up or down the number of replicas of your test application, and verify that the cluster can handle the changes in workload.

```
# Scale up the number of replicas
kubectl   scale   deployment   <deployment-name>   --replicas
<replicas>

# Scale down the number of replicas
kubectl   scale   deployment   <deployment-name>   --replicas
<replicas>
```

By following these steps, you can test the setup of your Kubernetes cluster across the AWS, GCP, and Azure platforms and ensure that it is working as expected.

Recipe#6: Writing Deployment Configuration YAML Files

Understanding YAML Files

YAML (YAML Ain't Markup Language) is a human-readable data serialization language that is often used to write configuration files. It is designed to be easy to read and write, and to be able to represent complex data structures in a way that is both simple and intuitive.

YAML files use a set of rules and conventions to represent data in a hierarchical structure. They use indentation to denote nesting, and use various indicators to denote the type of data being represented, such as strings, numbers, lists, and dictionaries.

Following is a sample program of a simple YAML file that represents a list of people and their ages:

```
---
- name: Alice
  age: 25
- name: Bob
  age: 30
- name: Charlie
  age: 35
```

YAML files are commonly used in Kubernetes to specify configuration for applications and services, as well as to define the structure of other resources in the cluster. They are also used in many other systems and tools to represent configuration data.

Writing Deployment Configuration Files

Deployment configuration files in Kubernetes are written in the YAML format and are used to specify how an application or service should be deployed to a Kubernetes cluster. Following is a sample program of a deployment configuration file that you might use to deploy a simple web server to a cluster:

```
apiVersion: apps/v1
kind: Deployment
metadata:
  name: webserver
  labels:
    app: webserver
spec:
  replicas: 2
  selector:
```

```yaml
  matchLabels:
    app: webserver
  template:
    metadata:
      labels:
        app: webserver
    spec:
      containers:
      - name: webserver
        image: nginx:latest
        ports:
        - containerPort: 80
```

This configuration file specifies that the deployment should create two replicas of the web server, using the nginx image and exposing port 80. The deployment is labeled with the app: webserver label, which is used to identify the replicas and connect them to other resources in the cluster.

To deploy this application to a cluster, you can use the kubectl command line tool:

```
# Deploy the application to the cluster
kubectl apply -f webserver-deployment.yaml
```

You can then check the status of the deployment using the kubectl tool:

```
# Check the status of the deployment
kubectl get deployments
```

This is just a simple example of a deployment configuration file, but you can use similar YAML files to specify more complex deployments with multiple containers, volumes, secrets, and other resources.

Recipe#7: Setting Up Load Balancers

Need of Load Balancers

Load balancers are systems that distribute incoming network traffic across a group of servers or other resources. They are commonly used to improve the performance, reliability, and scalability of web applications and other networked services.

Load balancers can be implemented in hardware, software, or as a combination of both. They typically work by receiving incoming network traffic and forwarding it to one of the available servers or resources based on a set of rules or algorithms. The load balancer can also monitor the health of the servers and resources and redirect traffic away from any that are not responding correctly.

Load balancers can be used in many different contexts, such as to balance traffic between multiple web servers, to distribute traffic among multiple databases, or to route traffic to different servers based on the type of request or the location of the client.

In Kubernetes, load balancers can be used to expose services to external clients, or to distribute traffic among different pods or replicas within the cluster. Kubernetes provides various mechanisms for creating and managing load balancers, including the Service resource and the Ingress resource.

Steps to Establishing and Configuring Load Balancers

Following are some helpful steps you can follow to establish and configure load balancers in your system:

- Identify the need for a load balancer. Determine whether you need a load balancer and, if so, what type of load balancer is appropriate for your needs. Consider factors such as the type of traffic you need to balance, the number of servers or resources you need to balance, and the performance and reliability requirements of your system.
- Choose a load balancer solution. Select a load balancer solution that meets your needs and is compatible with your infrastructure. Options may include hardware load balancers, software

load balancers, or cloud-based load balancers.

- Set up the load balancer. Install and configure the load balancer according to the instructions provided by the vendor. This may involve configuring the load balancer's network settings, setting up its connection to the servers or resources it will be balancing, and configuring the load balancing rules and algorithms.
- Test the load balancer. Test the load balancer to ensure that it is working as expected and that it is properly distributing traffic among the servers or resources. This may involve generating traffic and monitoring the load balancer's performance and behavior.
- Monitor and maintain the load balancer. Monitor the load balancer to ensure that it is performing well and to identify and resolve any issues that may arise. Perform regular maintenance and updates to keep the load balancer running smoothly.

Installing and Configuring Load Balancers Using HAProxy

Following is a sample program on how you might establish and configure a load balancer in your system using the popular open-source software load balancer, HAProxy:

- Install HAProxy on a server or virtual machine that will act as the load balancer. You can install HAProxy using your system's package manager or by downloading the source code and compiling it manually.

```
# Install HAProxy on Ubuntu or Debian
apt-get update && apt-get install haproxy

# Install HAProxy on CentOS or Fedora
yum update && yum install haproxy
```

- Configure the load balancer. Edit the HAProxy configuration file to specify the servers or resources that the load balancer should balance, as well as the load balancing algorithm and other settings.

```
# Edit the HAProxy configuration file
```

```
nano /etc/haproxy/haproxy.cfg

# Add the following lines to the file to balance traffic
between two servers
frontend http-in
  bind *:80
  default_backend servers

backend servers
  balance roundrobin
  server server1 192.168.0.100:80 check
  server server2 192.168.0.101:80 check
```

- Start the load balancer. Use the systemctl command to start the HAProxy service and enable it to start automatically on boot.

```
# Start the HAProxy service
systemctl start haproxy

# Enable the HAProxy service to start automatically on boot
systemctl enable haproxy
```

- Test the load balancer. Generate some traffic to the load balancer and verify that it is distributing the traffic among the servers or resources as expected. You can use the haproxy command line tool to check the status of the load balancer and its connections.

```
# Check the status of the load balancer
haproxy -c -f /etc/haproxy/haproxy.cfg

# Check the status of the connections to the servers
haproxy -c -f /etc/haproxy/haproxy.cfg -s show servers state
```

- Monitor and maintain the load balancer. Use tools such as systemctl, haproxy, and log files to monitor the performance of the load balancer and identify any issues that may arise. Perform regular maintenance and updates to keep the load balancer running smoothly.

```
# Check the status of the HAProxy service
systemctl status haproxy

# View the HAProxy log files
tail -f /var/log/haproxy.log
```

This is just a simple example of how you might establish and configure a load balancer using HAProxy, but you can use similar techniques to set up and manage load balancers using other software or hardware solutions.

Recipe#8: Setting Up Monitoring and Logging with Prometheus and Grafana

Installing and Configuring Prometheus

Prometheus and Grafana are popular open-source tools for monitoring and logging systems and applications. Following is a sample program on how you might set up monitoring and logging using these tools:

- Install and configure Prometheus. Download and install the Prometheus server and configure it to scrape metrics from the systems and applications you want to monitor. You will need to specify the target systems and the metrics you want to collect in the Prometheus configuration file.

```
# Download the Prometheus binary
wget
```

```
https://github.com/prometheus/prometheus/releases/download/
v2.21.0/prometheus-2.21.0.linux-amd64.tar.gz

# Extract the Prometheus binary
tar xvf prometheus-2.21.0.linux-amd64.tar.gz

# Change to the Prometheus directory
cd prometheus-2.21.0.linux-amd64

# Edit the Prometheus configuration file
nano prometheus.yml

# Add the following lines to the file to scrape metrics from
a server
scrape_configs:
  - job_name: 'server'
    static_configs:
      - targets: ['192.168.0.100:9100']
```

Installing and Configuring Grafana

- Install and configure Grafana. Download and install the Grafana server and configure it to connect to the Prometheus server. You will need to specify the URL and credentials for the Prometheus server in the Grafana configuration file.

```
# Download the Grafana binary
wget https://dl.grafana.com/oss/release/grafana-7.5.3.linux-
amd64.tar.gz

# Extract the Grafana binary
tar xvf grafana-7.5.3.linux-amd64.tar.gz

# Change to the Grafana directory
```

```
cd grafana-7.5.3

# Edit the Grafana configuration file
nano conf/defaults.ini

# Add the following lines to the file to connect to the
Prometheus server
[datasources.yaml]
datasources:
  - name: Prometheus
    type: prometheus
    url: http://prometheus:9090
    access: proxy
    isDefault: true
```

- Start the Prometheus and Grafana servers. Use the systemctl command to start the Prometheus and Grafana services and enable them to start automatically on boot.

```
# Start the Prometheus service
systemctl start prometheus

# Enable the Prometheus service to start automatically on
boot
systemctl enable prometheus

# Start the Grafana service
systemctl start grafana-server

# Enable the Grafana service to start automatically on boot
systemctl enable grafana-server
```

- Access the Grafana dashboard. Use a web browser to access the Grafana dashboard at http://<server-ip>:3000. You will need to log in using the default username and password, which are admin and admin, respectively.

- Configure monitoring and logging. Use the Grafana dashboard to create dashboards, panels, and alerts to monitor and log the metrics you are collecting from your systems and applications. You can use the Prometheus data source to create queries and visualize the metrics, and you can set up alerts to notify you when certain thresholds are exceeded or when there are other issues with your systems.

- Monitor and maintain the monitoring and logging system. Use tools such as systemctl, prometheus, and grafana-server to monitor the performance of the monitoring and logging system and identify any issues that may arise. Perform regular maintenance and updates to keep the system running smoothly.

CHAPTER 11: FUZZ TESTING AND STATIC ANALYSIS

Fuzz testing and static analysis are two techniques that can be used to improve the reliability and security of Rust programs.

Fuzz testing, also known as fuzzing, is a technique for testing the robustness of a program by providing it with invalid or unexpected input. The goal of fuzz testing is to find bugs and vulnerabilities that might not be discovered through normal testing.

There are a number of tools and libraries available for fuzz testing in Rust, such as cargo-fuzz and libfuzzer-sys. These tools allow you to define a target function that takes a byte slice as input, and then generate and provide random or semi-random input to the function in order to test its behavior.

Static analysis is a technique for analyzing the code of a program without actually running it. The goal of static analysis is to find potential issues, such as bugs, security vulnerabilities, and code style issues, by examining the code itself.

There are a number of tools and libraries available for static analysis in Rust, such as clippy and rust-analyzer. These tools allow you to check your code for a variety of issues, including syntax errors, unused variables, and potential security vulnerabilities.

Using both fuzz testing and static analysis can help you catch issues early in the development process, before they become problems in production. Both techniques can be integrated into your testing and development workflow, and are an important part of creating robust and reliable Rust programs.

Recipe#1: Identify The Target System

To begin fuzz testing in Rust, you need to identify the target system that you want to test. The target system is the part of your program that you want to test using fuzzing.

Steps to Follow for Identification of Target System

There are a few steps you can follow to identify the target system for your fuzz testing:

- Identify the functions or methods in your program that are most likely to be affected by invalid or unexpected input. These might include functions that parse input from external sources, such as a file or network connection, or functions that handle user input.

- Determine the input format for the target system. This might be a file format, network protocol, or other data structure.

- Define the input and output data types for the target system. For example, if the target system is a function that parses a file, you might define the input as a byte slice and the output as a struct or other data type that represents the parsed file.

- Write a wrapper function that takes a byte slice as input and calls the target system with the input. This wrapper function will be used as the target for the fuzz testing.

Once you have identified the target system and defined the input and output data types, you can use a fuzz testing tool, such as cargo-fuzz or libfuzzer-sys, to generate and provide random or semi-random input to the target system and check its behavior.

Use of cargo-fuzz to Perform Fuzzing

First, you will need to add the cargo-fuzz crate to your Cargo.toml file:

```
[dependencies]
cargo-fuzz = "0.6.8"
```

Next, define the target function that you want to test. This function should take a byte slice as input and return a result:

```rust
fn parse_input(input: &[u8]) -> Result<ParsedInput,
ParsingError> {
    // Parse the input and return the result
}
```

Then, create a new Rust project for your fuzz tests using the cargo fuzz command:

```
cargo fuzz init
```

This will create a new directory named fuzz in your project, with a file named fuzz_targets/fuzz_target_1.rs. This file contains a stub for the fuzz target function that you will need to fill in.

Define Wrapper Function to Call Target System

Add the following code to the fuzz_target_1.rs file to define the wrapper function that calls the target system:

```rust
#[fuzz_target]
fn fuzz_target(input: &[u8]) {
    match parse_input(input) {
        Ok(parsed) => {
            // Do something with the parsed input
        }
        Err(err) => {
            // Do something with the error
        }
    }
}
```

This wrapper function will be called with the input provided by the fuzzer. It calls the parse_input() function, which is the target system, and handles the result.

Finally, use the cargo fuzz run command to run the fuzz tests:

```
cargo fuzz run fuzz_target_1
```

This will run the fuzz tests using the fuzz_target_1 wrapper function as the target. The fuzzer will generate and provide random or semi-random input to the wrapper function, and the wrapper function will call the target system with that input. The fuzzer will then check the output of the target system to see if it behaves as expected.

You can customize the behavior of the fuzzer by passing various options to the cargo fuzz run command. For example, you can specify the number of inputs to generate, the length of the inputs, or the seed value to use for generating the inputs. You can also specify additional wrapper functions to run as separate fuzz targets.

Recipe#2: Identify Inputs

Understand The Format of The Input

To begin identifying inputs for fuzz testing in Rust, you need to first understand the format of the input that the target system expects. This will typically depend on the specific function or method that you are testing, as well as any external factors that may affect the input, such as file formats or network protocols.

Once you have a good understanding of the input format, you can start brainstorming ideas for inputs to test. Some ideas for inputs to test might include:

Valid input that is within the normal range of values that the target system expects. This can help you ensure that the target system is able to handle valid input correctly.

Invalid input that is outside the normal range of values that the target system expects. This can help you test the robustness of the target system and ensure that it can handle invalid input without crashing or returning incorrect results.

Input that is larger or smaller than the target system is designed to handle. This can help you test the performance of the target system and ensure that it can handle large or small inputs efficiently.

Malformed input that is intentionally designed to cause issues in the target system. This can help you test the security of the target system and ensure that it is resistant to attacks such as buffer overflows or injection attacks.

It's important to note that the specific inputs that you test will depend on the characteristics of the target system and the goals of your testing. You may need to test a wide range of inputs in order to thoroughly test the target system.

Once you have identified a list of inputs to test, you can use a fuzz testing tool, such as cargo-fuzz or libfuzzer-sys, to generate and provide the inputs to the target system and check its behavior. The fuzzer will typically generate and provide a large number of inputs in a short period of time, which can help you identify issues that might not be discovered through manual testing.

Identify Inputs with cargo-fuzz

To identify inputs for fuzz testing with cargo-fuzz, you can use a combination of manual and automated techniques.

One way to identify inputs is to manually create a list of inputs that you want to test. You can do this by understanding the format of the input that the target system expects and brainstorming ideas for inputs to test, as I described earlier.

Once you have a list of inputs, you can use cargo-fuzz to generate and provide the inputs to the target system and check its behavior. To do this, you will need to define a wrapper function that takes a byte slice as input and calls the target system with the input. You can then use the #[fuzz_target] attribute to mark the wrapper function as a fuzz target, and use the cargo fuzz run command to run the fuzz tests.

In addition to manually creating a list of inputs, you can also use cargo-fuzz to automatically generate inputs for you. To do this, you can use the corpus feature of cargo-fuzz, which allows you to define a set of "seed" inputs that the fuzzer will use to generate additional inputs.

To use the corpus feature, you will need to create a directory named corpus in the fuzz directory of your project, and add the seed inputs as files in the corpus directory. The fuzzer will then use these seed inputs to generate additional inputs and provide them to the target system.

You can also use the cargo fuzz add command to add additional seed inputs to the corpus. This can be useful if you want to add inputs that are generated by the target system itself, or if you want to add inputs that are based on specific scenarios or test cases.

Using the corpus feature can help you identify inputs that are particularly effective at finding issues in the target system, and can help you focus your testing efforts on the most important inputs.

Recipe#3: Generate Fuzzed Data

What Is Fuzzed Data

Fuzzed data is data that has been intentionally modified or generated in a way that is designed to test the limits of a program or system. It is often used to find vulnerabilities or defects in software by providing inputs that the developers may not have anticipated. Fuzzed data can take many forms, depending on the specific goals of the fuzzing process and the characteristics of the program or system being tested. Some common types of fuzzed data include random data, modified versions of valid inputs, and invalid or malformed inputs.

In the context of cargo-fuzz, the fuzzed data is generated by the function defined in the fuzz_targets.rs file. This function takes a mutable reference to a byte slice as its only argument, and can modify the contents of the slice to create the fuzzed data. The resulting data is then used as input for the program being tested.

Use of cargo-fuzz to Generate Fuzzed Data

To generate fuzzed data with cargo-fuzz, you will need to do the following:

- Install cargo-fuzz by running cargo install cargo-fuzz.
- Create a new Rust project by running cargo new --bin fuzz-project.
- In the fuzz-project directory, create a new directory called fuzz.
- In the fuzz directory, create a new Rust file called fuzz_targets.rs. This file will contain the functions that cargo-fuzz will use to generate inputs for your program.
- Define a function in fuzz_targets.rs that takes a mutable reference to a byte slice as its only argument. This function will be used to generate the fuzzed inputs for your program.

Following is a sample program on a simple fuzz target function:

```rust
#[fuzz_target]
fn my_fuzz_target(data: &mut [u8]) {
    let s = std::str::from_utf8(data).unwrap();
    println!("{}", s);
}
```
In the fuzz-project directory, create a file called fuzz/Cargo.toml with the following contents:

```toml
[package]
name = "fuzz-project"
version = "0.1.0"
authors = ["Your Name <your@email.com>"]

[lib]
name = "fuzz_targets"
```

```
crate-type = ["cdylib"]

[dependencies]
cargo-fuzz = "0.6.6"
```

Run cargo fuzz run my_fuzz_target to start the fuzzing process. Cargo-fuzz will use the my_fuzz_target function to generate and test inputs for your program.

Recipe#4: Best Practices to Run Fuzzing

Best Practices to Run Fuzz Testing

Following are some helpful best practices for running fuzz testing in Rust:

- Use a tool like cargo-fuzz to automate the fuzzing process. Cargo-fuzz makes it easy to set up and run fuzz tests, and it integrates seamlessly with the Rust ecosystem.

- Define clear goals for your fuzz testing efforts. What are you trying to achieve with your fuzz tests? are you looking for specific types of vulnerabilities, or are you just trying to get a general sense of the robustness of your code? Having clear goals will help you design your fuzz tests more effectively.

- Define robust and well-defined fuzz target functions. Your fuzz target functions should be able to handle a wide range of inputs and should be resistant to panic or other types of failures.

- Use cargo-fuzz's coverage-guided fuzzing feature to focus your efforts on the most important parts of your code. Coverage-guided fuzzing uses code coverage information to prioritize the testing of parts of your code that are less well-tested, which can help you find defects more efficiently.

- Use Rust's built-in testing features, such as the #[test] attribute, to write unit tests for your code. These tests can provide a baseline of correctness against which to compare the results of your fuzz tests.

- Monitor the results of your fuzz tests carefully, and pay particular attention to any panics or other unusual behavior. If you find a defect or vulnerability, consider writing a unit test to reproduce it and then fixing the issue.

- Consider using a tool like cargo-fuzz-build to build your fuzz targets in release mode, which can improve the performance of your fuzz tests and help you find defects more quickly.

- Use Rust's type system to your advantage when designing your fuzz target functions. For example, consider using types like &[u8] or &str to represent inputs, rather than raw pointers or other low-level types. This can help you avoid common pitfalls like null pointers and out-of-bounds memory accesses.

- Use the no_std feature to disable the Rust standard library and minimize the attack surface of your fuzz targets. This can make it more difficult for attackers to exploit vulnerabilities in your code and can also improve the performance of your fuzz tests.

- Consider using a tool like cargo-fuzz-profiler to profile your fuzz tests and identify performance bottlenecks. This can help you optimize your code and make your fuzz tests run more efficiently.

Recipe#5: Checking Syntax Errors

Various Techniques to Identify Syntax Errors

There are several techniques that you can use to check for syntax errors in Rust programs:

- Use the Rust compiler to check for syntax errors. The Rust compiler will automatically check your code for syntax errors and other issues when you build your program. If it finds any problems, it will display an error message that describes the issue and suggests possible solutions.

- Use a Rust-specific text editor or integrated development environment (IDE) that includes support for Rust syntax highlighting and error checking. Many IDEs and text editors include built-in support for Rust, and some even include features like automatic formatting and code completion to make it easier to write correct Rust code.

- Use a linter tool like clippy to check for syntax errors and other issues in your Rust code. Linters can help you find problems with your code that the Rust compiler might not catch, such as style issues or potential runtime errors.

- Write unit tests for your code. Unit tests can help you ensure that your code is correct and free of syntax errors by testing specific parts of your program in isolation.

- Use static analysis tools like miri to check for syntax errors and other issues in your Rust code. Static analysis tools can help you find problems with your code by analyzing it at compile time, rather than waiting until runtime.

Executing Techniques to Spot Syntax Errors

Here's a brief overview of how to use each of the techniques I listed to identify syntax errors in Rust programs:

- Use the Rust compiler to check for syntax errors:

- To check for syntax errors using the Rust compiler, you can simply run the cargo build or cargo check command in your project's directory. If the compiler finds any syntax errors or other issues, it will display an error message that describes the problem and suggests possible solutions.

- Use a Rust-specific text editor or IDE:

- Many text editors and IDEs include support for Rust syntax highlighting and error checking. For example, if you're using the Visual Studio Code editor, you can install the Rust (rls) extension to get syntax highlighting and error checking for your Rust code. To check for syntax errors in an IDE, simply open your Rust code in the editor and look for any error messages that are displayed by the editor.

- Use a linter tool like clippy:

To use clippy to check for syntax errors in your Rust code, you will need to install it first. You can do this by running the following command:

```
cargo install clippy
```

Once clippy is installed, you can run it by running the cargo clippy command in your project's directory. If clippy finds any issues with your code, it will display an error message that describes the problem and suggests possible solutions.

- Write unit tests for your code:

To write unit tests for your Rust code, you will need to use the #[test] attribute to mark your test functions. For example:

```
#[test]
fn test_function() {
    // test code goes here
}
```

To run your tests, you can use the cargo test command. If any of your tests fail, it may indicate a syntax error or other issue with your code.

- Use static analysis tools like miri:

To use miri to check for syntax errors and other issues in your Rust code, you will need to install it first. You can do this by running the following command:

```
cargo install miri
```

Once miri is installed, you can run it by running the cargo miri command in your project's directory. If miri finds any issues with your code, it will display an error message that describes the problem and suggests possible solutions.

Recipe#6: Detecting Coding Style Issues

Various Techniques to Detect Flaws In Coding Styles

There are several techniques that you can use to detect flaws in coding styles in Rust programs:

- Use code review tools like CodeScene or LGTM to review your code and identify coding style issues. Code review tools can help you catch problems with your code that you might have missed, and they can also help you improve your coding style by suggesting best practices and alternative approaches.
- Follow established coding standards and guidelines for Rust, such as the Rust style guidelines or the Rust API guidelines. Adhering to these standards can help you write consistent and maintainable code.

Use of CodeScene and LGTM to Improve Coding Styles

CodeScene and LGTM are code review tools that can help you identify issues with your code and improve your coding style. Here's a brief overview of how to use these tools:

- Sign up for an account with CodeScene or LGTM. Both tools offer free accounts for open source projects.
- Install the appropriate integration for your text editor or IDE. CodeScene and LGTM offer integrations for a variety of popular text editors and IDEs, including Visual Studio Code, IntelliJ, and Eclipse.
- Configure the integration to point to your code repository. CodeScene and LGTM can be used with a variety of code hosting platforms, including GitHub, GitLab, and Bitbucket.
- Use the code review tool to review your code and identify issues. Both CodeScene and LGTM offer a variety of features to help you review your code, including syntax highlighting, error checking, and code metrics.
- Use the suggestions and recommendations provided by the code review tool to improve your code. Both CodeScene and LGTM offer suggestions for best practices and alternative approaches that can help you improve your coding style.

Use of Rust Style Guidelines to Avoid Coding Style Issues

The Rust style guidelines are a set of recommendations for writing consistent and maintainable Rust code. They are intended to help developers write code that is easy to read and understand, and that follows best practices for Rust development.

Some key points covered by the Rust style guidelines include:
- Naming conventions: The Rust style guidelines recommend using snake case for variable and function names, and using mixed case for module and type names.
- Formatting: The Rust style guidelines recommend using four spaces for indentation, and placing curly braces on the same line as the preceding statement.
- Code structure: The Rust style guidelines recommend organizing code into small, focused functions and keeping functions short and simple.
- Documentation: The Rust style guidelines recommend using Rust's built-in documentation syntax to write clear and concise documentation for your code.
- Annotations: The Rust style guidelines recommend using attributes like #[cfg] and #[warn] to provide additional information about your code and help ensure that it is compiled correctly.

These are just a few of the recommendations covered by the Rust style guidelines. for a complete list of guidelines, you can refer to the official Rust style guide, which is available at https://doc.rust-lang.org/1.52.0/style/.

Recipe#7: Identifying Security Vulnerabilities

Techniques to Find Security Vulnerabilities

There are several techniques that you can use to find security vulnerabilities in Rust projects:
- Use a static analysis tool like miri or clippy to find potential vulnerabilities in your code.

These tools can help you identify problems with your code that might lead to security vulnerabilities, such as null pointers or uninitialized variables.

- Use a dynamic analysis tool like cargo-fuzz to find vulnerabilities by running your code with a wide range of inputs. Fuzz testing can help you find vulnerabilities by providing inputs that the developers may not have anticipated and that could potentially cause the program to crash or behave unexpectedly.

- Use a code review tool like CodeScene or LGTM to review your code and identify potential security vulnerabilities. Code review tools can help you catch problems with your code that you might have missed, and they can also suggest best practices and alternative approaches that can help improve the security of your code.

- Follow established security guidelines and best practices for Rust development. There are many resources available that can help you learn about best practices for writing secure Rust code, such as the Rust security guidelines or the Rust API guidelines.

- Use unit tests and other testing techniques to ensure that your code is robust and resistant to attacks. By testing your code thoroughly, you can help ensure that it is less likely to have security vulnerabilities.

Using Static Analysis Tool, 'Miri' to Spot Vulnerabilities

To use miri to find vulnerabilities in your Rust code, you will need to install it first. You can do this by running the following command:

```
cargo install miri
```

Once miri is installed, you can use it to analyze your code for potential vulnerabilities by running the cargo miri command in your project's directory. miri will then analyze your code and look for potential issues that could lead to security vulnerabilities, such as null pointers or uninitialized variables.

If miri finds any issues with your code, it will display an error message that describes the problem and suggests possible solutions. For example, if miri finds an uninitialized variable, it might display an error message like this:

```
error: uninitialized variable: `x`
  --> src/main.rs:4:5
   |
4  |         let y = x + 1;
   |           ^
```

To fix this issue, you can initialize the variable x with a value before using it in your code.

CHAPTER 12: CODE PERFORMANCE OPTIMIZATION

There are several ways that Rust developers can optimize code performance:

Use profiling tools: Rust has several tools that can help you identify performance bottlenecks in your code. These include perf, valgrind, and flamegraph. You can use these tools to measure the time and resources that your code consumes and identify areas that may be causing performance issues.

Use optimization flags: Rust has several optimization flags that you can use to improve the performance of your code. These flags can be passed to the Rust compiler when you build your code, and they can help the compiler generate faster and more efficient code.

Use efficient data structures: Choosing the right data structure for your code can have a significant impact on its performance. Rust has several data structures that are optimized for different use cases, such as Vec for dynamic arrays and HashMap for fast key-value lookups.

Avoid unnecessary allocations: Allocating memory on the heap can be expensive, especially if it happens frequently. Try to minimize the number of allocations that your code performs, or consider using a data structure that avoids allocations altogether, such as a Vec with a fixed capacity.

Use unsafe code sparingly: Rust's safety guarantees come at a performance cost, so using unsafe code can sometimes give you a performance boost. However, it's important to use unsafe code carefully and only when it's necessary, as it can also introduce vulnerabilities into your code if used incorrectly.

Consider using a faster programming language: In some cases, you may be able to achieve better performance by using a different programming language that is better suited to your specific use case. Languages like C and C++ are often used for performance-critical applications, but they may not offer the same level of safety and reliability as Rust.

Use parallelism: If your code is CPU-bound, you may be able to improve its performance by using parallelism. Rust has several built-in features for parallelizing code, such as the rayon crate and the parallel iterator.

Use SIMD instructions: If your code performs a lot of arithmetic on large arrays of data, you may be able to improve its performance by using Single Instruction Multiple Data (SIMD) instructions. Rust has built-in support for SIMD through the simd crate.

Use low-level optimizations: If you need to squeeze every last bit of performance out of your code, you may need to use low-level optimization techniques. This could include things like manually unrolling loops, inlining functions, or using assembly code.

Use external libraries: If you need to perform a specific task that requires a lot of performance, you may be able to find an external library that is optimized for that task. For example, the blaze crate is a high-performance library for parsing and serializing data.

Optimize your algorithm: Finally, one of the most effective ways to optimize code performance is to optimize the algorithm that your code is using. This could involve using a faster algorithm, reducing the number of calculations that your code performs, or minimizing the amount of data that your code has to process.

Recipe#1: Identify Performance Bottlenecks Using 'perf'

What Is 'perf' Tool?

perf is a performance analysis tool for Linux systems. It allows you to measure the performance of a program by recording a trace of its execution and generating a report of the data that was collected. perf can be used to profile a wide range of performance characteristics, including CPU usage, memory access patterns, and I/O operations.

perf is a powerful tool that can provide detailed insights into how a program is using resources and where performance bottlenecks may be occurring. It is commonly used by developers to optimize the performance of their code, but it can also be used by system administrators to troubleshoot performance issues on a Linux system.

perf is included with most modern Linux distributions and is typically run from the command line. It has a wide range of options and features that allow you to customize the data that is collected and the way that it is presented.

Running 'perf' Tool and Recording Performance Report

To identify performance bottlenecks using perf in Rust, you'll need to install the perf tool on your system. On most Linux systems, you can do this by running sudo apt-get install linux-tools-common.

Once perf is installed, you can use it to profile a Rust program by running the following command:

```
perf record -g -- <program_name> <program_arguments>
```

This will run your Rust program and record performance data, including information about function call stacks and the time that each function takes to execute.

After your program has completed, you can generate a report of the performance data by running:

```
perf report
```

This will generate a report that shows the time that each function in your program took to execute, as well as the number of times that each function was called. You can use this information to identify functions that are taking a long time to execute or are being called frequently, which may indicate a performance bottleneck.

You can also use the perf tool to profile specific functions or regions of code. For example, you can use the -f flag to specify a function to profile, or the -j flag to profile a specific set of threads.

Recipe#2: Analyze Performance Bottlenecks Using 'valgrind'

What Is Valgrind?

valgrind is a tool for debugging and profiling programs, primarily on Linux systems. It can be used to identify and analyze a wide range of issues in a program, including memory leaks, invalid memory accesses, and performance bottlenecks.

In Rust, valgrind can be used to identify issues with memory management and to help optimize the performance of a program. To use valgrind with a Rust program, you'll need to install it on your system (on most systems, you can do this by running sudo apt-get install valgrind) and then run your program through valgrind using the following command:

```
valgrind --tool=memcheck <program_name> <program_arguments>
```

This will run your Rust program and collect data about its memory usage and any errors that it encounters. After the program has completed, valgrind will generate a report that shows the results of the analysis. You can use this report to identify any issues with your program's memory management or to find performance bottlenecks that may be caused by inefficient memory usage.

Analyzing Performance Bottlenecks Using 'valgrind'

Here are the steps you can follow to analyze performance bottlenecks using valgrind with a Rust program:

- Install valgrind on your system: If you don't already have valgrind installed, you'll need to install it first. On most Linux systems, you can do this by running sudo apt-get install valgrind.

- Compile your Rust program with debug symbols: valgrind relies on debug symbols to provide detailed information about your program's execution. To enable debug symbols in your Rust program, you'll need to compile it with the --debug flag. For example:

```
rustc --debug <program_name>.rs
```

- Run your program through valgrind: To analyze your program's performance using valgrind, you'll need to run it through the valgrind tool. You can do this using the following command:

```
valgrind --tool=memcheck <program_name> <program_arguments>
```

This will run your program and collect data about its memory usage and any errors that it encounters.

- Review the valgrind report: After your program has completed, valgrind will generate a report that shows the results of the analysis. You can use this report to identify any issues with your program's memory management or to find performance bottlenecks that may be caused by inefficient memory usage.

For example, you can look for lines in the report that indicate that your program is allocating and deallocating a large amount of memory, as this could indicate a performance bottleneck. You can also look for lines that indicate that your program is accessing memory in an invalid or unsafe manner, as this could indicate a bug in your code.

- Optimize your code based on the report: Once you've identified the issues that are causing performance bottlenecks in your code, you can work to fix them. This may involve changing the way that your program manages memory, using more efficient data structures, or optimizing your algorithms.

Recipe#3: Running Different Optimization Flags

What are Optimization Flags In Rust?

Optimization flags are compiler options that can be used to improve the performance of a Rust program. These flags instruct the Rust compiler to generate faster and more efficient code, at the cost of potentially longer compile times and larger binary sizes.

Different Types of Optimization Flags

There are several different types of optimization flags in Rust, including:
- -O: This flag enables basic optimization techniques, such as inlining small functions and removing unused code.
- -O1: This flag enables additional optimization techniques beyond those enabled by -O, such as loop unrolling and function inlining.
- -O2: This flag enables even more aggressive optimization techniques, including global value numbering and interprocedural optimization.
- -O3: This flag enables the most aggressive optimization techniques available, including link-time optimization and profile-guided optimization.

To use optimization flags in Rust, you can pass them to the compiler when you build your program. For example, to build a Rust program with basic optimization enabled, you can use the following command:

```
rustc -O <program_name>.rs
```

You can also specify multiple optimization flags to enable more aggressive optimization. For example:

```
rustc -O2 -O3 <program_name>.rs
```

Keep in mind that using optimization flags can increase the compile time of your program and result in larger binary sizes. You should use them sparingly and only when performance is a critical concern.

How to Implement Optimization Flags In Rust Programs?

Following is a sample program on how you can use optimization flags in a sample Rust program:

- Write your Rust program: First, you'll need to write your Rust program. for this example, let's assume that your program is called main.rs and it contains the following code:

```
fn main() {
    println!("Hello, world!");
}
```

- Compile your program with optimization flags: To build your program with optimization flags, you'll need to pass the flags to the rustc compiler when you build your program. For example, to build your program with basic optimization enabled, you can use the following command:

```
rustc -O main.rs
```

This will generate an optimized executable file called main in the same directory.

- Run your program: To run your optimized program, you can simply execute the generated executable file:

```
./main
```

This will run your program and print "Hello, world!" to the console.

You can also specify multiple optimization flags to enable more aggressive optimization. For example:

```
rustc -O2 -O3 main.rs
```

This will build your program with both -O2 and -O3 optimization flags enabled. It's also a good idea to test your program with different optimization levels to find the right balance between performance and compile time. You can use the --emit=llvm-ir flag to output the LLVM intermediate representation (IR) of your program and compare the generated IR with different optimization levels to see how the compiler is transforming your code.

Recipe#4: Using SIMD Instructions for Efficient Performance

Understanding SIMD Instructions

Single Instruction Multiple Data (SIMD) instructions are a type of processor feature that allows a CPU to perform the same operation on multiple pieces of data simultaneously. SIMD instructions can be used to improve the performance of code that performs a lot of arithmetic on large arrays of data, such as image processing or scientific simulations.

Single Instruction Multiple Data (SIMD) instructions can provide several benefits for Rust applications, including:

- Improved performance: SIMD instructions can greatly improve the performance of code that performs a lot of arithmetic on large arrays of data, such as image processing or scientific simulations. By allowing the CPU to perform the same operation on multiple pieces of data simultaneously, SIMD instructions can significantly reduce the number of instructions that the CPU needs to execute, which can result in significant performance improvements.

- Efficient use of CPU resources: SIMD instructions can help to make better use of the CPU's resources by allowing it to perform more work in parallel. This can help to reduce the CPU's idle time and improve overall system performance.

- Reduced code complexity: Using SIMD instructions can often simplify the code that you need to write to perform arithmetic on large arrays of data. For example, instead of writing a loop to perform arithmetic on each element of an array individually, you can use SIMD instructions to perform the same operation on multiple elements at once.

- Portability: The simd crate provides a portable and convenient way to access SIMD instructions from Rust, allowing you to write code that can take advantage of SIMD instructions on any processor that supports them.

What Is 'simd' Crate?

The simd crate is a Rust library that provides safe and convenient access to Single Instruction Multiple Data (SIMD) instructions on processors that support them. SIMD instructions are a type of processor feature that allows a CPU to perform the same operation on multiple pieces of data simultaneously, which can greatly improve the performance of code that performs a lot of arithmetic on large arrays of data.

The simd crate provides a set of types that represent SIMD vectors and functions for manipulating them. For example, the i32x4 type represents a SIMD vector containing four 32-bit integers, and the + operator can be used to perform vector addition. The simd crate also provides functions for loading and storing SIMD vectors from and to arrays, as well as functions for performing common operations such as element-wise addition and multiplication.

Here's a simple example of how you can use the simd crate to perform efficient vector arithmetic on an array of integers:

```rust
use simd::{i32x4, u32x4};

fn main() {
```

```rust
    let mut a = [1, 2, 3, 4, 5, 6, 7, 8];
    let b = [10, 20, 30, 40, 50, 60, 70, 80];

    // Load the arrays into SIMD vectors
    let a_vec = i32x4::from_slice_unaligned(&a);
    let b_vec = i32x4::from_slice_unaligned(&b);

    // Perform vector arithmetic
    let c_vec = a_vec + b_vec;

    // Store the result back in the array
    c_vec.write_to_slice_unaligned(&mut a);

    println!("{:?}", a); // prints [11, 22, 33, 44, 55, 66, 77, 88]
}
```

Using the simd crate in this way can greatly improve the performance of code that performs a lot of arithmetic on large arrays of data. However, it's important to note that SIMD instructions are only available on certain processors.

Using 'simd' Crate In Rust Application

Following is a sample program on how you can use the simd crate to perform efficient vector arithmetic on an array of integers:

```rust
use simd::{i32x4, u32x4};

fn main() {
    let mut a = [1, 2, 3, 4, 5, 6, 7, 8];
    let b = [10, 20, 30, 40, 50, 60, 70, 80];

    // Load the arrays into SIMD vectors
```

```rust
    let a_vec = i32x4::from_slice_unaligned(&a);
    let b_vec = i32x4::from_slice_unaligned(&b);

    // Perform vector arithmetic
    let c_vec = a_vec + b_vec;

    // Store the result back in the array
    c_vec.write_to_slice_unaligned(&mut a);

    println!("{:?}", a); // prints [11, 22, 33, 44, 55, 66, 77, 88]
}
```

In this example, the i32x4 type represents a SIMD vector containing four 32-bit integers. We use the from_slice_unaligned function to load the arrays a and b into SIMD vectors, and then use the + operator to perform vector addition. Finally, we use the write_to_slice_unaligned function to store the result back in the array a.

Using SIMD instructions in this way can greatly improve the performance of code that performs a lot of arithmetic on large arrays of data.

Recipe#5: Overcoming Style Violations

Different Types of Style Violations

In Rust programming, style violations refer to deviations from the Rust community's recommended style guidelines. These guidelines are designed to help Rust programmers write code that is easy to read, understand, and maintain, and are based on the Rust Language Design Guidelines and the Rust API Guidelines.

There are many different style guidelines for Rust programs, covering topics such as naming conventions, formatting, comments, and documentation. Some common style violations in Rust programs include:

- Incorrect naming of variables, functions, and types
- Inconsistent use of formatting and indentation
- Lack of or incorrect documentation for functions and types
- Incorrect use of comments
- Inconsistent use of whitespace and punctuation

Steps to Remove Style Violations

There are several steps you can follow to remove style violations from your Rust programs:

- Identify the style violations. Use tools such as rustfmt and clippy to scan your code for style violations and identify the specific areas that need to be fixed. These tools can often automatically fix some style violations, but others may require manual intervention.
- Fix the style violations. Review the identified style violations and make the necessary changes to your code to fix them. This may involve renaming variables, functions, and types, adjusting formatting and indentation, adding or updating documentation, and making other changes as needed.
- Run the style checker again. After making the necessary changes, run the style checker again to ensure that all style violations have been fixed. If there are still style violations remaining, repeat the process until all violations have been addressed.
- Review the changes. Review the changes you have made to your code to ensure that they are correct and that your code is now compliant with the recommended style guidelines. This may involve reviewing the changes with other team members or using code review tools and practices.

By following these steps, you can remove style violations from your Rust programs and help ensure that your code is consistent with the recommended style guidelines. Remember to regularly run the style checker to catch any new style violations as you work on your code, and to review your code to ensure that it is readable, understandable, and maintainable.

Using 'rustfmt' and 'clippy' to Remove Style Violations

Install rustfmt and clippy. Use cargo, the Rust package manager, to install rustfmt and clippy on your system.

```
# Install rustfmt
cargo install rustfmt

# Install clippy
cargo install clippy
```

Identify the style violations. Use rustfmt and clippy to scan your code for style violations. For example, you can use the following command to run rustfmt on your code:

```
# Run rustfmt on the current directory
rustfmt .
```

This will scan your code and report any style violations it finds. You can use the --check flag to have rustfmt report the violations without making any changes to your code.

```
# Check for style violations without making any changes
rustfmt --check .
```

Similarly, you can use the following command to run clippy on your code:

```
# Run clippy on the current directory
cargo clippy
```

This will scan your code and report any style violations or other issues that clippy finds.

Fix the style violations. Review the style violations reported by rustfmt and clippy, and make the necessary changes to your code to fix them. rustfmt can often automatically fix some style violations, but others may require manual intervention. clippy can provide suggestions for how to fix certain issues, but it may not always be able to automatically fix them.

Run the style checker again. After making the necessary changes, run rustfmt and clippy again to ensure that all style violations have been fixed. If there are still style violations remaining, repeat the process until all violations have been addressed.

Review the changes. Review the changes you have made to your code to ensure that they are correct and that your code is now compliant with the recommended style guidelines. This may involve reviewing the changes with other team members or using code review tools and practices.

Following is a sample program on how you might fix a style violation in your Rust code using rustfmt:

```
# Initial code with a style violation
fn foo() {
    let x = 10;
    let y = 20;
}

# Code after running rustfmt
fn foo() {
    let x = 10;
    let y = 20;
}
```

As you can see, rustfmt has automatically fixed the style violation by adjusting the formatting and indentation of the code.

Similarly, Following is a sample program on how you might fix an issue identified by clippy:

```
# Initial code with an issue identified by clippy
```

```
fn main() {
    let mut x = 10;
    x += 1;
    println!("{}", x);
}


# Code after running clippy and making the suggested changes
fn main() {
    let x = 10;
    let x = x + 1;
    println!("{}", x);
}
```

In this example, clippy has identified an issue with the += operator and has suggested using the + operator instead. By making this change, the issue has been resolved.

By following these steps and using tools such as rustfmt and clippy, you can remove style violations from your Rust programs and help ensure that your code is consistent with the recommended style guidelines. Remember to regularly run the style checker to catch any new style violations as you work on your code, and to review your code to ensure that it is readable, understandable, and maintainable.

Recipe#6: Use of Low-Level Optimization Techniques

Understanding Low-Level Optimization Techniques

Low-level optimization techniques in Rust are techniques that involve making changes to the underlying hardware or operating system in order to improve the performance of a Rust program.

These techniques can be useful when the performance of your program is critical and you need to squeeze every last bit of performance out of your system. However, low-level optimization techniques can also be complex and time-consuming, and they may involve making trade-offs between performance and other factors such as reliability, security, and maintainability.

Some examples of low-level optimization techniques in Rust include:

- Using unsafe code: Rust has a strong emphasis on safety, but sometimes you may need to use unsafe code in order to achieve the highest possible performance. unsafe code allows you to bypass Rust's safety checks and perform operations that would otherwise be prohibited, such as directly manipulating memory or calling foreign functions.
- Tuning the memory allocator: The memory allocator is responsible for managing the allocation and deallocation of memory in your program. By tuning the memory allocator, you can improve the performance of your program by reducing the overhead of allocating and deallocating memory.
- Using specialized data structures: Some data structures are designed to be faster or more memory-efficient than others. By using specialized data structures, you can improve the performance of your program by reducing the time and space complexity of your algorithms.
- Using SIMD instructions: SIMD (Single Instruction Multiple Data) instructions allow you to perform multiple operations in parallel using a single instruction. By using SIMD instructions, you can improve the performance of your program by making better use of the hardware's capabilities.

Benefits of Low-Level Optimization Techniques

There are several benefits to using low-level optimization techniques in Rust:

- Improved performance: The main benefit of low-level optimization techniques is that they can help improve the performance of your Rust program. By making changes to the underlying hardware or operating system, you can often achieve significant performance improvements that would not be possible using higher-level techniques.
- Greater control: Low-level optimization techniques give you greater control over the behavior of your program, allowing you to fine-tune the performance of your code in ways that are not possible with higher-level techniques.

- Better use of hardware: Low-level optimization techniques can help you make better use of the hardware's capabilities, allowing you to get more out of your system and potentially reduce hardware costs.

- Reduced complexity: In some cases, using low-level optimization techniques can help reduce the complexity of your code, making it easier to understand and maintain. For example, using specialized data structures or SIMD instructions can often lead to more concise and efficient code.

However, it is important to carefully consider the trade-offs involved when using low-level optimization techniques. These techniques can be complex and time-consuming, and they may involve making trade-offs between performance and other factors such as reliability, security, and maintainability. It is important to make sure that the benefits of using low-level optimization techniques outweigh the costs.

Using Low-Level Optimization Techniques In Rust Programs

Following are some helpful examples of how low-level optimization techniques might be used in a Rust program:

Using unsafe code: unsafe code can be used to bypass Rust's safety checks and perform operations that would otherwise be prohibited, such as directly manipulating memory or calling foreign functions. For example, you might use unsafe code to implement a high-performance sorting algorithm:

```rust
unsafe fn quicksort(arr: &mut [i32]) {
    if arr.len() <= 1 {
        return;
    }

    let pivot = partition(arr);
    quicksort(&mut arr[..pivot]);
    quicksort(&mut arr[pivot + 1..]);
```

```rust
}

unsafe fn partition(arr: &mut [i32]) -> usize {
    let pivot = arr.len() / 2;
    arr.swap(pivot, arr.len() - 1);

    let mut i = 0;
    for j in 0..arr.len() - 1 {
        if arr[j] < arr[arr.len() - 1] {
            arr.swap(i, j);
            i += 1;
        }
    }

    arr.swap(i, arr.len() - 1);
    i
}
```

Tuning the memory allocator: You can tune the memory allocator by adjusting its parameters or by using a different allocator altogether. For example, you might use the jemalloc allocator, which is known for its high performance:

```rust
extern crate jemallocator;

#[global_allocator]
static            ALLOC:           jemallocator::Jemalloc            =
jemallocator::Jemalloc;
```

Using specialized data structures: You can use specialized data structures to improve the performance of your program by reducing the time and space complexity of your algorithms. For example, you might use the hashbrown crate to implement a hash map:

```rust
use hashbrown::HashMap;
```

```rust
let mut map = HashMap::new();
map.insert("foo", 10);
map.insert("bar", 20);
```

Using SIMD instructions: You can use SIMD instructions to perform multiple operations in parallel using a single instruction. For example, you might use the simd crate to implement a vector addition function:

```rust
use simd::{i32x4, i32x4_add};

fn add_vectors(a: &[i32], b: &[i32]) -> Vec<i32> {
    assert_eq!(a.len(), b.len());

    let mut result = Vec::with_capacity(a.len());
    let mut i = 0;

    while i < a.len() {
        let a_chunk = i32x4::from_slice_unaligned(&a[i..i + 4]);
        let b_chunk = i32x4::from_slice_unaligned(&b[i..i + 4]);
        let c_chunk = i32x4_add(a_chunk, b_chunk);
        result.extend_from_slice(c_chunk.as_slice());
        i += 4;
    }

    result
}
```

These are just a few examples of how low-level optimization techniques might be used in a Rust program. It is important to carefully consider the trade-offs involved when using these techniques and to make sure that the benefits of using them outweigh the costs. It is also important to remember that low-level optimization techniques are just one tool in the toolbox, and that in many cases, higher-level optimization techniques such as algorithmic optimization or code refactoring may be more effective at improving the performance of your program.

Following are some helpful additional resources that may be helpful in learning more about low-level optimization techniques in Rust:

- The Rust Programming Language book: https://doc.rust-lang.org/book/
- The unsafe guide: https://doc.rust-lang.org/stable/unstable-book/language-features/unsafe.html
- The alloc crate: https://doc.rust-lang.org/stable/alloc/index.html
- The hashbrown crate: https://docs.rs/hashbrown/
- The simd crate: https://docs.rs/simd/
- The num_cpus crate: https://docs.rs/num_cpus/

Recipe#7: Utilizing External High Performance Libraries

List of External High Performance Libraries In Rust

There are many external high-performance libraries available for Rust that can help you improve the performance of your programs. Here are a few examples:

- jemalloc: A high-performance memory allocator that can improve the performance of your program by reducing the overhead of allocating and deallocating memory.
- hashbrown: A fast and memory-efficient implementation of a hash map.
- rayon: A library for parallel programming that can help you take advantage of multi-core processors.

- simd: A library for using SIMD instructions to perform multiple operations in parallel using a single instruction.

- num_cpus: A library for detecting the number of CPUs available on a system.
- scoped-threadpool: A library for creating a pool of threads that can be used to execute tasks in parallel.
- rayon-core: A low-level library for parallel programming that provides a foundation for other parallelism libraries.

These are just a few examples of the many high-performance libraries available for Rust. It is worth exploring the available libraries and determining which ones are most appropriate for your needs. Some libraries may be better suited for certain types of tasks or hardware architectures, so it is important to carefully consider your specific requirements when choosing a library.

Utilizing High Performance Libraries In Rust Programs

Following is a sample program on how you might use some of the high-performance libraries listed above in a Rust program:

jemalloc: To use jemalloc as your memory allocator, you can add the following to your Cargo.toml file:

```
[dependencies]
jemallocator = "0.3"
```

Then, in your Rust code, you can use the jemallocator crate to set jemalloc as the global allocator:

```
extern crate jemallocator;

#[global_allocator]
static ALLOC: jemallocator::Jemalloc = jemallocator::Jemalloc;
```

hashbrown: To use hashbrown as your hash map implementation, you can add the following to your Cargo.toml file:

```
[dependencies]
hashbrown = "0.9"
```

Then, in your Rust code, you can use the HashMap type from the hashbrown crate:

```
use hashbrown::HashMap;

let mut map = HashMap::new();
map.insert("foo", 10);
map.insert("bar", 20);
```

rayon: To use rayon for parallel programming, you can add the following to your Cargo.toml file:

```
[dependencies]
rayon = "1.6"
```

Then, in your Rust code, you can use the par_iter method to execute a closure in parallel over the elements of a collection:

```
use rayon::prelude::*;

let v = vec![1, 2, 3, 4, 5];

let result = v.par_iter().sum();

println!("{}", result); // 15
```

simd: To use simd to perform SIMD instructions, you can add the following to your Cargo.toml file:

```
[dependencies]
simd = "0.4"
```

Then, in your Rust code, you can use the types and functions provided by the simd crate to perform SIMD operations:

```rust
use simd::{i32x4, i32x4_add};

fn add_vectors(a: &[i32], b: &[i32]) -> Vec<i32> {
    assert_eq!(a.len(), b.len());

    let mut result = Vec::with_capacity(a.len());
    let mut i = 0;

    while i < a.len() {
        let a_chunk = i32x4::from_slice_unaligned(&a[i..i +
4]);
        let b_chunk = i32x4::from_slice_unaligned(&b[i..i +
4]);
        let c_chunk = i32x4_add(a_chunk, b_chunk);
        result.extend_from_slice(c_chunk.as_slice());
        i += 4;
    }

    result
}
```

scoped-threadpool: To use scoped-threadpool to create a pool of threads, you can add the following to your Cargo.toml file:

```
[dependencies]
scoped-threadpool = "0.1"
```

Then, in your Rust code, you can create a ScopedThreadPool and use it to execute tasks in parallel:

```rust
use scoped_threadpool::Pool;

let pool = Pool::new(4);

pool.scoped(|scoped| {
    for i in 0..10 {
        scoped.execute(move || {
            println!("Hello from thread {}", i);
        });
    }
});
```

rayon-core: To use rayon-core for low-level parallel programming, you can add the following to your Cargo.toml file:

```toml
[dependencies]
rayon-core = "1.7"
```

Then, in your Rust code, you can use the types and functions provided by the rayon-core crate to execute tasks in parallel:

```rust
use rayon_core::{join, join_context, spawn, ThreadPool};

let pool = ThreadPool::new(4).unwrap();

let handle = pool.spawn(|| {
    println!("Hello from a new thread!");
});

handle.join().unwrap();
```

These are just a few examples of how you might use some of the high-performance libraries listed above in a Rust program.